CW00515733

The Criminal Mind in the Age of Globalization

The Criminal Mind in the Age of Globalization

By

SARON MESSEMBE OBIA

Vij Books India Pvt Ltd
New Delhi (India)

Published by

Vij Books India Pvt Ltd
(Publishers, Distributors & Importers)
2/19, Ansari Road
Delhi – 110 002
Phones: 91-11-43596460, 91-11-47340674
Mob: 98110 94883
E-mail: contact@vipublishing.com
Web : www.vijbooks.in

Copyright © 2021, *Author*

ISBN: 978-81-94697-40-4 (Hardback)

ISBN: 978-81-94697-41-1 (Paperback)

ISBN: 978-81-94697-42-8 (ebook)

All rights reserved.

No part of this book may be reproduced, stored in a retrieval system, transmitted or utilized in any form or by any means, electronic, mechanical, photocopying, recording or otherwise, without the prior permission of the copyright owner. Application for such permission should be addressed to the publisher.

The views expressed in this book are of the contributors/authors in their personal capacity.

Dedicated to

To almighty God and Mr. Sammy Sammy Obia

CONTENTS

Acknowledgement xi

Introduction 1

CHAPTER ONE

Cybercrime, Identity Theft and Identity Fraud

Typology of Crimes 7

The Changing Character of Crime in Africa 9

The Modus Operandi of Cybercriminals 12

Categorization and Profiling of Cyber Criminals 15

Theoretical Analysis 19

Challenges of Criminal Investigations 23

A Review of Best Practices For Developing Countries 26

CHAPTER TWO

Deviance in the Cyber Age

Social Media and Deviance 35

Landscape of social media and deviant behavior 35

Cyber election interference in U.S 36

The press as a model of construct and destabilization: the
Cameroon example 40

The French and Danish examples 43

Cyber deviance in the music industry 44

Sexual deviance on social media 47

Cyberbullying on social media 49

Theoretical analysis of the freshman suicide case 53

Sanctions and severity of social networking sites 55

Facebook as case study 55

CHAPTER THREE

Biometric System and Digital Forensics

Biometric Classification 59

Biometric Patterns For Organizations 60

Biometric Strategy For States 61

Forensics Investigation And Biometrics 63

Theoretical Framework of Forensic investigation 67

Emerging trends of cybercrime and identity theft

Cybercriminal pattern through mobile money 72

Scholarship Scam 76

Non-governmental organizations; a new paradigm
for cybercriminals 77

Financial crime and identity theft 77

CHAPTER FOUR

Prostitution and Cyber Insecurity in Cameroon

Cyber Insecurity Scenery 80

The Role of Prostitutes in Cyber criminality in Cameroon 81

Hacking of accounts and skimming 81

Mobile Money Accounts (MMA) 83

An examination of financial crimes in Nigeria   85

Drug, offensive content and harassment   86

CHAPTER FIVE

Cyber Terrorism, Cyberattack and Radicalism

Cyberterrorism Theory   91

The Globalization Era   93

Challenges involved in combating cybercrime and
terrorist activities   94

Terrorist Financing   96

The Internet as an Open Source Information Tool
for Terrorist Attacks   97

Identity & Attribution   99

References   107

Index   127

ACKNOWLEDGEMENT

I would like to acknowledge Dr. Dan Ekongwe, Regional Director of the Pan African Institute for Development, West Africa-Buea and Dr. Celestina Fru Tassang for their invaluable guidance in my academic research. As a researcher in criminology trained in Cameroon and product of an international and diplomatic institution, the Pan African Institute for Development, West Africa (PAID-WA). I am very fortunate to have spent the past one and half years on a different trajectory in the field of security studies. As a result, I feel confident to approach security issues from all dimensions.

I would also like to express my sincere appreciation to Noor Dahri, Founder and Executive Director of the Islamic Theology of Counter Terrorism (ITCT), United Kingdom, who has been of assistance, to Colonel (Rtr) Youssa Gedeon (PhD), Major (Rtr) Dieudonne Bilec, Commissaire Principale (Rtr) Siewe Levir, Mr Martin Hale, CEO IT Masters, Adjunct Senoir Lecturer at Charles Sturt University (CSU) for the knowledge acquired through his educational platform, Sir Andrin Raj (PhD), Director of the International Association for Counter Terrorism and Security Professional South East Asia (IACSP SEA), Tammy Waitt, Editorial Director of American Security Today, and also to Mr. Tchouksonou Jean Marie. I am grateful to Madam Tchouksonou Pamela Bessong, National Pedagogic Inspector for Bilingualism in Cameroon, for her linguistic expertise.

I am deeply honored to have received positive and encouraging feedback from Philomena O'Grady, Forensic Criminologist, whose insight was impactful, Rev. Ngalle Simon, Mr. Pendie Kelvin N., Mr. Wilson Mengole, Mr. Prospere Baihoul, Mr. Abraham K. Mendy,

Mr. Fandjio Mougang B. and from Hon. Elizabeth Mokake, whose advice led me into the field of international security. I am also indebted to the legendary Prof. Bishop Jatau Emmanuel of Faith Hills Prophetic Assembly, Abuja/ Nigeria for both his professional advice and his personal kindness.

INTRODUCTION

This work provides insight to criminal investigators and the criminal justice system on the necessity for collaboration with financial institutions, security expert and mobile service providers on how to crack down cybercriminals. Chapter one provides an insight of cybercrime, identity theft and identity fraud. It explores the various types of crimes, the sociology of crimes in Africa, modus operandi, practical illustrations with the triangular theory of crimes and the constructive theory. The challenges of criminal investigations are enormous, pertinent case studies are explained following new trends. It further elaborates on best practices for developing countries in the field of cyber security.

"Information is money but intelligence breach equates war". Social networking sites are increasing used for socio-political probes in the world. Chapter two explores deviant attitudes on the cyber space. First it draws in to the concept of social media and deviant behavior on the internet, focusing on emerging threats and the cyber election interference in the United States of America. The menace posed by social media in developing countries and particularly in former French colonies. Cameroon is a critical case at hand, where the press has a double identity; that is as an element of construct and destabilization. It also examines cyber deviance in the music industry with case of Nigeria and Cameroon, as well as sexual deviance in University milieu, cyberbullying on social media. The chapter through a theoretical in-depth explores the neutralization theory and sanctions impose by social networking sites with Facebook as case study.

In the field of security studies, one plus one does not equate two. Despite the evolution of information technology, biometric

1

system and digital forensics demurs a formidable fop in criminal investigations. Chapter three examines the ideology of criminal investigators using biometric system and digital forensics to track cybercriminals. Biometric classification and organization pattern are being explored, as well as strategies use by some states. The chapter points out the different trends for criminal crack down. Also, the 5 stages of cybercrime and three stage model of cyber criminality are being exploited for a proper theoretical framework. The chapter provides emerging crimes and challenges for proper security measures to establish through exchange of security intelligence amongst regional and international agencies in the fight against non-conventional crimes.

Chapter four is reminiscent to a published article on cyber criminality and prostitution in Cameroon. The existence of legislations does not limit prostitution and it is critically linked to cybercrime. Chapter four illustrates how profit demurs the prime reasons for mobile operating companies, security measures neglected and staff dishonesty in financial institutions. The inadequate expertise in relation to cyber security and lack of understanding of criminal patterns is another dilemma. The chapter describes a prostitute as one of the major partners of cybercriminals during the commission of crimes. From the cyber insecurity scenery, the role of prostitutes is examined, hacking of accounts and skimming as well as, contemporary crimes as mobile money account breach. It further examines illicit drug consumption, offensive content and harassment even in university milieus.

The 9/11 attacks gave a different narrative about international security; lack of collaboration amongst security agencies. There are several security challenges that exist, such as; global intelligence organizations, civil aviation organizations and the international criminal police. Chapter five examines the increasing nature of cyber terrorism, cyberbullying and radicalization in Europe, Middle East and part of Africa. This transnational order is explained by the new cyber terrorism theory. The June 2014 General Assembly review of the United Nations put forth 4 pillars in combatting terrorism. The future of security is perpendicular, as sovereignty free actors (terrorist) continue to aspire to stage attacks through wires, and coordinated attacks through 'flying birds' (drones and planes). This chapter investigates the cultural clash between the 'west' and some religious fundamentalists in the Middle East and part of Africa, not forgetting their financing source. The globalization era facilitates terrorist patterns as identity theft is another pin to divert intelligence profiling, the Umar Farouk A. case is being examined to better understand some of the threats posed to the U.S military machine. The chapter caps with the UN 4 pillars in combatting global terrorism.

CHAPTER ONE

CYBERCRIME, IDENTITY THEFT AND IDENTITY FRAUD

The internet is a global tool for the transfer of information by individuals, organizations and governments.[1] The evolution from manual to digital information technology (internet) involves the use of e-commerce whose activities involve online sales of different commodities and the delivery of different services (ATM, Monetary transfers) across the globe. Aunshul Rege defines cybercrime as any crime related to information and communication technology used by an agent or perpetrator to swill victim from savings, it is either a single attack or on-going series of events.[2] Identity theft or identity fraud is a practice of stealing personal information (person's name, social security number, driver's license, birth date or credit card numbers) and pretending to be that person in order to obtain financial resources in that person's name without consent.[3] Technological advancements in terms of the cyberspace in Africa, has produced shifts in the ability to reproduce, distribute, control and publish information, the internet in particular has changed the economics of production and reproduction (Longe and Chiemeke, 2008).

---

1 S, Obia. (2018) Cybercrime and Identity Theft. A Practical Guide for Cameroon Police. Lambert Academic Publishing.

2 Also see; O. Adel "Catching Up With The Rest Of The World: The Legal Framework Of Cybercrime In Africa", Media and Technology Law, ongoing – UNSW , Pg 2

3 Agbor, A. (2016). Cyber Criminality as a Crime in Cameroon. University of Buea, Cameroon (unpublished thesis)

Due to the complexity of internet activities and the scope of different practices within the cyberspace of a country[4], it is important to expose the difference between a hacker and a cybercriminal. According to Misha Glenny[5], the difference between a cybercriminal and a hacker is that a cybercriminal is someone who indulges in illegal activities on the internet for financial motives, whereas a hacker is one that breaches into a computer system of an individual, organization or government institution without authorization. The hacker either seeks to steal information files or cause damage to data. On the other hand, a hacker can become a cybercriminal even though the two individuals are categorized as cyber criminals. With such challenges to expertise, there is, therefore, the need for African stakeholders to strengthen the avenues and develop the skills of personnel involve in the control, management and supervision of the cyber space[6]. Such actions will facilitate control, management, examination and evaluation of cybercrimes and particularly the means to track perpetrators of these crimes.

Since the lack of expertise (technological and educational expertise) is invariably attached to the lack of evidence during proceedings in the Criminal Justice System[7]. The lack of evidence is a major challenge to track and render justice against cybercrimes due to the complexity of the crime. Cyber criminals mutate their strategies to hide the pattern of cybercrime from policing and the Criminal Justice System. For example, a pedophile who baits his victim through email or social networks. This delays the decision-making process thereby delaying the punishment and this can also lead to wrong decisions encouraging other criminals to be casual and fearless. Furthermore, the hacking of the Cameroon presidential website in 2015, makes such reinforcement and search for effective

---

4   Odumesi, J. (2014) point the rule of law as one of the major factors in combatting cyber criminality despite the challenges and complex nature.

5   Watch Misha Glenny's interview on 'Profiling cybercrime' YouTube

6   Akuta et al (2011) posed that, law enforcement officers engaged in the fight against cyber criminality are not usually computer literates and have not be trained in cyber security during the passage at the police academy.

7   Aluko (2004)

expertise as well as the development of a criminal database and an upgraded version of the internet an urgent proposition.

From the foregoing, the difficulty to identify, disrupt, dismantle and prosecute cybercriminals has become a major security challenge to African countries. The evolution of technology has become complex and technically advanced, such that these non-conventional crimes demand innovative security expertise and operations because advances in technological system and software have created a gap between the security personnel services and the criminals whose research have shown that they continue to outpace the authorities due to their better mastery of the internet.

When the security develops understanding of a pattern or profile of cybercrimes, the cybercriminals adopt different and innovative means of operation as well as complex dispositions to operate, such as change of Internet Protocol (IP) address.[8] This is due to their constancy and age frequency to the new technologies and internet operation systems[9]. The increasing number of registered cases and complaints from victims of cyber criminality, appeals for proper solution in combatting its threat.

Typology of Crimes

Carders or card cloned: Stealing bank or credit card details is another major cybercrime. Duplicate cards are then used to withdraw cash at ATMs or in shops.

Malware: Malware is software that takes control of any individual's computer to spread a bug to other people's devices or social networking profiles. Such software can also be used to create a

---

8   There are two types of IP'S; Internet protocol version 4 (IPV4 or V4) use on packet switched networks and also includes Transmission Control Protocol (TCP). The second is Internet protocol version 6 (IPV6 or V6) the communications protocol that provides an identification and location system for computers on networks and routes traffic across the Internet

9   The Cameroonian President Paul Biya during his end of year speech to the nation describes youths as the Android generation (CRTV, 2016)

'botnet' a network of computers controlled remotely by hackers, known as 'herders,' to spread spam or viruses[10].

Internet dating and romance scam: The paradigm of cybercriminals in Cameroon has change the dynamics of international and national security. As crimes keep evolving with on various social networks like Facebook[11], cougars and even oasis, women are more seen on Facebook. With the quest to find a foreigner (bush faller)[12] that would take them out of Cameroon through marriage or invitation to the resident country.

Phishing: Phishing involves cybercriminals posing as reputable organizations or businesses in order to obtain confidential information from their victims. This is often carried out through sending emails or utilizing phony website. An example of this is where victims are asked to enter their login details on "bank" websites where they are then redirected to the fake website allowing the cybercriminals to then record their information. Phishing (sometimes called carding or brand spoofing) is often linked to identity fraud. Financial and personal details obtained fraudulently from victims are used to gain access to funds and this has cost businesses and financial institutions billions of dollars.

Cyberstalking: Cyberstalking is the use of the internet to harass an individual, an organization or a specific group. There are many ways in which cyberstalking becomes cybercrime. Cyberstalking involves monitoring of someone's activity real-time, via an electronic device online, and while offline. Cybercrime becomes a crime because of the repeated threatening, harassing or monitoring of someone with whom the stalker has, or no longer has a relation.

---

10 See Professor Prashant Sharma's presentation on relationship between Cybercrime and Engineering. https://www.slideshare.net/PrashantSharma215/cyber-crime-and-cyber-security-52327084

11 Ibid 1 also read; (Virkus, 2008) and (Social Bakers, 2013)

12 Bushfallers is word used to describe Africans living in Europe and Western continent. They are usually considered to be rich and ladies in Africa, will quickly connect to such a people.

Cyberstalking can include harassment of the victim, the obtaining of financial information of the victim or threatening the victim in other to frighten them. An example of cyberstalking would be to put a recording or monitoring device on a victim's computer or smartphone in order to save envy keystroke they may make so that the stalker can obtain information. Another example would be repeatedly posting derogatory or personal information about a victim on web pages and social media despite being warned not to do so.

The Changing Character of Crime in Africa

The changing pattern of crime can be described as the sociology of crime and addresses questions about the emergence of new patterns and the rise of different categories of crimes in society. The sociology of crime examines the manifestation of diverse crime structures such as violence and deviant behaviour and the responses to it. Durkheim E. has observed that crime, violence and deviant behaviour are linked to community welfare and development[13]. Violence and crime therefore affect every dimension of man's social existence from a social, political and historical perspective and are not new phenomena in the field of development theory[14]. According to Rogers (1989) the link between violence, crime and societal development is historic and can be traced to urbanization and underdevelopment (security) in the developing countries. For instance, Africa is viewed as the most violent continent based on crime victimization rates followed by Latin America (UNICRI, 1995; UNCHS, 1996).

Violence as a particular crime can be described as an action or word that is intended to hurt someone or the extreme use of force that leads to an attack on someone. Violence or violent conduct is a situation or event in which an individual, people or an organization is hurt or killed. In the sociology of knowledge,

---

13 Dr. Daneil Ekongwe (2015), during his lectures of sociology of crimes, explains reason why youths get engage in to certain cultures. Also see; NordiskaAfrkainstitutet (2001) ASSOCIATIONAL LIFE IN AFRICAN CITIES: Popular Responses to the Urban Crisis.

14 Ibid 7.

violence is considered as a global public health problem that can be explained psychologically and scientifically.

The psychological explanation about violence turns around the argument that humans are biological creatures who although operate at animal level are more superior to other animals[15]. However, there is evidence that violent behaviour is caused by physical action which originates from the stimulation of the brain. The biological aggressive tendency is triggered by some psychological mechanism linked to the human brain. On the other hand, the scientific evidence explaining violent behaviour or the physical argument on violence is linked to substances that can cause a dramatic change in some one's behaviour.

However, the unprecedented increase of violence in the 21st century can be linked to technology which is increasingly at the service of hate ideologies, deviance and cybercrimes as new dimensions of criminal behaviour. There are more evidence of violence in the life of individuals such as child abuse by their parents and tutors; women injured or humiliated by violent partners (Bekali, E., 2017); elderly persons maltreated by caretakers; youth violence and self-inflicted violence because the victims learn from their victimizers. New generations learn from the past as well as social conditions that nurture violence.

Some research has argued that to avoid violence it's important to stay indoors, or lock doors and windows to avoid dangerous people and places. However, escaping from violence is not possible by locking oneself indoors because of technology and the exploration of cyber space that allows the penetration of every boundary or barrier to prevent violence. For instance, the threat of violence behind those closed doors such as child abuse, violence on wives by their partners and those in war and conflict zones can be breached through the internet (internet or cyber bullying).

Another pattern of crime is deviant behaviour. Deviance can be defined as behaviour that violates expected rules and norms and it is more than nonconformity. Sociologists who study deviance

---

15 Dr. Daniel Ekongwe (2015) lecture notes on child development and evolution.

and crime examine cultural norms and how they change over time, how they are enforced and what happens to individuals and societies affected by deviance. It is behaviour that departs significantly from social expectations, such as the contemporary behaviour of youths stripping down their trousers or piecing their body parts. Sociologists like Charles Darwn continue to stress the social context and not just individual behavior when considering deviance. The study of deviance looks at why people violate laws or norms and the study of how society reacts to such non-conformist tendencies or attitude such as cybercrimes and the search for wealth by youths. The societal reaction to deviant behaviour suggests that social groups actually create deviance by making the rules whose infraction constitutes deviance and by applying those rules to particular people and labeling them as outsiders. In this regard, Robert Merton looks at deviance as innovative behaviour.

Robert K. Merton discusses deviance in terms of goals and means that is, as part of strain and anomie theory while Emile Durkheim states that anomie is the confounding of social norms. However, Robert Merton further states that anomie is the state in which social goals (youth search for quick wealth) and the legitimate means to achieve them do not correspond. Merton equally postulated that, an individual's response to societal expectations and the means by which the individual pursued those goals are suitable in understanding deviance. Relating to this study the understanding is therefore that the youth's wanton search for quick wealth through fraud is not a legitimate answer to youth bulge, unemployment, poor education or poverty. He observes that deviant action is motivated by strain, stress, or frustration in individuals and arises from a disconnection between the society's goals and the means to achieve those goals. The problem from a sociological stand point in this study would therefore be to deal with the social context in which behaviors such as cybercrimes are committed. Using 'innovation' which includes technology like the internet, Robert Merton describes the terms of acceptance and rejection of social goals and the institutionalization of achieving them.

11

Robert Merton argues that 'innovation' is a response to the strain generated by the cultural emphasis on the acquisition of wealth and the lack of opportunities to achieve it; the quest to get rich and the lack of the means to get rich. This causes people and particularly youths in Cameroon[16] like in other parts of the world, to be innovators and thereby engage in illegal activities that are considered deviant, such as stealing, cybercrimes, violence and thugry. By Mertons observations, innovators like the youths cybercriminal minds therefore, accept society's goals but reject the socially acceptable means of achieving them such as monetary success gained through crime.

Merton claims that innovators are those who have socialized with similar world views (the internet world or Android generation) but who have been denied the opportunities they need to be able to legitimately achieve society's goals. The continuous innovation of technology has therefore led to the changing form and patterns of crime from conventional to non-conventional crimes. Cybercrime began with 'scamming' whose outcome was that of easy money through fraudulent means, led to other innovative patterns and practices such as hacking and phishing. Today, there are new forms of crimes like skimming (using the Simbox for theft), Vishing (voice dialing), Smishing (SMS messaging) and cyber bullying[17]. The existence and evolution of these diverse and sophisticated online practices and the lack of effective expertise from public and judicial authorities has left a trail of victims in some African countries. The courts increasingly face the challenge of identifying and categorizing the crimes.

The Modus Operandi of Cybercriminals

The preliminary stages on the cyberspace

Information and communication technology has brought a variety of conventional crimes. Cyber criminality is one of the challenges to security officials. When the security officials make a step closer,

---

16 Abia et al (2010) provide some of the reasons why young Cameroonians engage in cybercrimes, identity theft and identity fraud.

17 Ibid

cyber criminals make ten steps further with the use of IP addresses and other terminal devices.[18] The language is also a barrier to the security as well as the society. We listen to new words each day, like machine man, Ngues man and pick-up, but there are also the ideas of bills in cyber criminality.[19] Here are the three main mails issued by cyber criminals;

Stage one on the cyberspace: Bill to be paid by victims[20]

The first mail or bill which constitutes all the description of the pets, feeding, toys and how he would be transported to the victim (Jk, Mugu, Maga).[21]

The second bill, the client how to process payment, should it be a bank to bank or simple transfer to local agencies. It should be noted, that there can be payment in the first bill if the person succumbs directly to the deal. Then the second bill would come in with a complaint of transportation fees and caging.

The third bill, the scammer comes in with the idea of insurance and medical assistance like vaccination or other drugs needed by the kitten.

Stage two on the cyber space: Behind the wires

With the experience of security experts, when transactions are made, precautions are also taken. They use protected protocols, emails and numbers. The connections they got sometimes give the law enforcement no opening. These are some of the methods;

---

18 Wacka, B. (2014) during a seminar on; Understanding and Investigating Cyber Criminality and Terrorist Acts. A Practical Approach for Law Enforcement Agents and the Judiciary, University of Buea, 13 November 2014

19 Cybercrime in Cameroon From 2009-2014 BY Saron Messembe Obia (unpublished manuscript)

20 Cybercriminals have three main bills depending on the type of scam. During an interview with some suspected cybercriminals, the later expose that bills depend on how the victim adhere to their product.

21 Jk, Mugu and Maga are words created by cybercriminals in the early 2000s to describe victims of non-conventional crimes (cybercrime, identity theft and identity fraud).

The use of a fake ID[22] card numbers to withdraw money, or create an account which only the scammer and the manager or cashier of the bank knows about. The process of obtaining ID cards is very easy, complaints of lost ID or a dishonest security staff provides a receipt that acts as an ID card with a fake name that does not exist. The manager or cashier of the financial institution helps delete any information of the transaction. The question is why does the victim not contact the security?

A pick-up[23]: This is a person found in a different state, which acts as a sale agent and receives the money before transacting it back to the scam. For instance if Baba scams Ines, he tell Ines to do the transfer to Texas, which his pick-up would receive, while collaborating with a person of the bank in Texas to erase the information. Though he may be using a nick name too, and send the money to Baba who is safe in a different country. That is how the security chain moves, the victim can't identify anybody, and because they are fake names and the pick-up also helps collaborate to delete the information at the bank at Texas.

The back- up by some insiders in communication network centers, there is always staff dishonesty. Certain workers would take the initiative of covering the network of cyber criminals in exchange for certain amounts of money. Law enforcement officers during investigations encounter some challenges following staff dishonesty with information request.[24] Thereby protecting criminals and with insufficient evidence.

---

22 Fake identity card (ID cards) or other documents use to perpetrate is termed 'docki' by cybercriminals.

23 The word Pick-up became popular in the late 2000s, when cybercriminals discovered that in order to divert funds, an individual can be used in the resident or foreign country protecting his identity from law enforcement tracking.

24 (CIFAS: 2012) argue, that staff dishonesty affects the organization, competing institutions and the community as well, and that the best way to fight crime is to have zero tolerance throughout the investigation.

Categorization and Profiling of Cyber Criminals

By this we explore the knowledge and understanding of the particular activities that facilitates the categorization of cybercrimes and which enhances the vital role of managing cybercrimes as an emergent security challenge. In shaping and prosecuting individuals, groups or governments involved in cyber criminality, the legislation along with the Penal Code when read harmoniously, should have sufficient evidence and knowledge of a particular cybercrime, the mutations in the activities as well as a critical understanding of the existence, form, nature, of the criminal behaviour.

The consensus in the sociology of knowledge about the evolution and categorization of crime and the process of identification of crime is called profiling. The essence is to consider and be able to effectively identify any one who engages in the practice of crime whose investigation can be facilitated by the exploitation of evidence or traces and patterns of the crime in order to draw a profile relevant to the security risk or tasks. This demands expert knowledge of the crime, the practice and the mechanics as well as the pathology of the exercise.

The theme of categorization and profiling here therefore examines the exploitation of traces and patterns of cyber criminality and the evolutionary criminal behaviour amongst Africans. The sub heading or theme is relevant because it will allow those with the responsibility of managing the challenge of cyber criminality to understand and have mastery of the crime circle in order to be able to gather and support evidence in their various security tasks concerning the use and misuse of the internet and online services. In terms of the challenge and lack of expertise the increase in knowledge and awareness in the wider sense can be linked to security, investigation, gathering of intelligence, surveillance or risk analysis.

The passion of users of the internet at the initial or early usage of the online service was to post information on the Facebook page or account, Tweet or exchange videos in chart rooms usually unaware of the dangers of their personal data. There has been a shift in these activities to include pornography and execute sale activities on the cyberspace for fame, profit and security breach of systems. As a result, the Criminal Justice System has taken interest in these activities as new and emerging crimes that increasingly involves the youths in most African countries. Despite this interest by the public authorities a number of challenges stand in their way to disrupt, dismantle or destroy the practices that include the procurement of evidence, lack of expertise in cyber criminality as well as institutional bottle-necks. In some cases the suspected criminals have actually been acquitted for the lack of evidence.[25]

The challenges that face the Criminal Justice System to prosecute suspects and effectively carry out justice for victims of cybercrimes can also be linked to career practices and development. In the legal profession a lawyer may change his career by training to become a judge. However, there is a general lack of interest and unwillingness by lawyers to become judges. More so, it has been reported about the failure to fill vacant High Court positions by the higher judicial authority. This has been explained to be the result of corruption and political appointments by the government. In his book titled "Civil Disobedience in Cameroon" (1992) A.N.T. Mbu explains that this practice has virtually destroyed the justice department in Cameroon.

The challenge of inaccessibility to criminals or the mapping and tracking of cybercriminals poses problems to the police because of the emerging cultures and development of groups or gangs describe as street culture which has change the mindset of some youths in Africa. The sophistry and development of these groups makes it difficult for the authorities to track them more so the groups make increasing use of sophisticated security tools and

---

25 See; The People of Cameroon vs. Che Valery Neba Holding at the High Court of Fako in Buea (2012) (HCF/085c/12) the case involved a gang or group of individuals who operated as a cybercriminal group. The facts of the case included the fraudulent acquisition and use of documents and the sale of black pepper to an online user. When the case was brought to the courtin Buea, the accomplices appeared in court as co-defendants. They included IkomYannick Njuh and Kenah Elias Wallang (unreported).

software like Hide My ASS for IP address whose sophistry is a problem to security officials. For example in Cameroon, ANTIC bemoaned this problem and lately is organizing training session for security and justice officials across the country through the program "Government IT, 2016."

The peak period of cyber criminality is the month of December when victims get into festive mood and want to buy pets and jewelries for their kins. According to records Russia tops the victim chart followed by the United States, Britain, Canada, France and Australia. However, the activities of high profile cybercriminals who deal in drugs, sale of vehicles, apartment blocks, land and other properties, is not seasonal.

Furthermore, the incidence of negligence and loopholes in a computer system of individuals, organizations or a state infrastructure or establishment can be protected against cybercrimes by risk analysis and assessment. Regular risk analyses and assessment are key items for combating cybercrime especially when authentication is properly done and certain sites restricted. This way ransom ware and attacks can be reduced. For instance, in 2011 the Federal Bureau of Investigation (FBI) disrupted a fraud operation based in Estonia whose activities had infected more than four million computers in 100 countries and stolen in excess of 14 million dollars from advertisement. Since workers have a low knowledge of Information Technology (IT) and a simple click can attract a spam which would automatically restart the system of the institution or organization thereby allowing full access or control of the system of the organization to hackers.

From a global perspective, it is important to note that technological globalization has facilitated the transfer of funds by banks across great distances, that is, from one country or region to another, in very short space of time. The activities of financial transaction and monetary transfer are no longer the prerogative of banks as there are many different financial institutions that are now involved in monetary transactions described as wiring between banks and countries and from one person to another.

Through the liberalization of the banking sector in Africa, such financial institutions now include micro-finances and financial houses like Western Union, Express Exchange, Express Union, MoneyGram, and Emi Money.[26] Their services are basically electronic funds transfer (EFT) and this allows banks and other financial institutions to transfer funds through computer signals over wires and telephone lines in very short space of time and great distances. During the transit period of the financial transaction the computer signals over wires and telephone lines can be interrupted by a hacker or be cracked. The sender would not be aware whether the transaction was successful or reached the intended destination because the hacker might have interfered with the transaction. This illegal operation is facilitated by the responds of individuals or first responders to unknown emails that enter the spam folder. Hackers operating as individuals or professionals attached to an organization take advantage of these unsuspecting individuals whose responses allow them access to their password.

The actions of hackers are also traceable to the activities of transnational companies and global actors who are increasingly active in the global market, service delivery and politics. In the discharge of their activities and services transnational companies create innovative programs which are introduced to global markets and customers. To have an insight of such innovative technologies or programs, professional hackers of competing firms are hired to crack the program for other organizations or multinationals in the same business or market such as the action between Apple and Microsoft. [27]

Furthermore, multinational and companies like hotels save huge amounts of personal data and details of their customers. When hackers gain access to the hotel system they have access to such files and collect personal information for their use in the criminal world.

---

26 Ibid 1

27 Ibid 1, P 23

In other situations dissatisfied employees or ex-employees can release clients and customer information that exposes credit card details and social security numbers. The level of understanding and knowledge of these practices is vital for individuals, groups, organizations and the state. It is therefore vital to have adequate or standard know how and expertise of information technology by those individuals and officials entrusted with the responsibility to disrupt, dismantle and destroy the hacking activities. As such, this study attempts to explain the typology and tools of cyber criminality in the tables below.

Theoretical Analysis

a) Triangular Theory of Crimes

The triangular theory is one of the recent and developing theories of cyber criminality describe the increasing nature of cyber-crime and identity theft on the African continent is because of the collaboration of criminals with the third party within and out of the Country. The theory exposes how financial transactions are pursued during and after victimization. Cyber criminality or cyber-crime is a confidential game, exploited by criminals through available opportunity and vulnerability. The theory relates cybercrime and identity theft to staff dishonesty, which is mostly exploited by cybercriminals to cover their identity[28]. That is, the criminals used fake identity cards and with the collaboration of staffs at financial institutions to modify, delete or fabricate information. The modus operandi as concerns cybercrime and identity theft goes as such; first the vulnerable (*Mugu, Maga and Jk*), who transfers funds to the pick-up in this case a (cashier, manager or any individual co-operating with the cybercriminal found in a different state or even the same resident state of the criminal), with the notion that the pick-up is the manager of existing company or organization as explained in the deal or agreement (bill) with his said client or agency. The pick-up then channels the money to the scammer described as (*dak man, machine man or Ngues man*) who intend receives the money in any of his resident areas, as a regular customer.

---

28 https://americansecuritytoday.com/triangular-theory-model-cybercrime/

The theory exposes how criminals protect their identity or avoid to be track by the police. This is because the criminal's real identity (name), resident area and mobile number are not revealed to the victim throughout the transaction (if any number of the name given is usually 25 fake). The theory reveals that this triangular transaction protects the identity of the criminal even from forensic investigations. The theory provides a plan action for law enforcement and security experts on how cybercriminals can equally receive a direct transfer to their account, in collaboration with the Manager or cashier Banks (*CODAC, Back-up*) of the bank or monetary institution. When the money is being withdrawn, the transfer detail is deleted, and the persons get involved in the transaction get his/her share. It should be noted that even certain agents in mobile operating companies also support (toolkit with unlimited credit, or give the password of profiled agents to cyber-criminals to browse with their identity) and cover cyber-criminals with different identities.

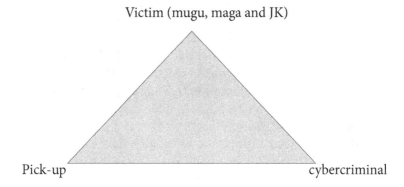

Victim (mugu, maga and JK)

Pick-up   cybercriminal

The Triangular theory

1. The level which cybercriminal data is evaluated in Cameroon. Law enforcement officers and security experts during investigations usually target only computers. Cybercriminals operate with other tools that are unidentifiable, like tablets, iPod without sim cards and cybercafé computers, making it difficult to identify the user.

2. An inadequate system of identification. The biometric ID card cannot effectively combat cyber-crime and identity theft. The

reason has been the inadequate security to stop skimming and hacking which has to do with financial institutions with biometric cards.

The relevance of this theory as concerns cybercrime and identity theft is to caution the law enforcement and security experts, as well as mobile operators and banks on the mutations of cybercrime and identity theft. Also, to educate on the emergence of a new language and the strategies adopted by cyber-criminals. This warrants censorship of the cyberspace, collaboration with telecommunication agencies, as well as financial institution scrutiny of a database system.

b) The constructive theory

The constructive theory is the reconceptualization of criminology theories which exposes illicit contracts and how fictitious companies operate online platforms which host photos of land for sale, award contracts and recruitment of workers in renowned companies, letter head of companies forged to win contracts, gather information of profiled individuals use to apply as sub-contractor, provide account statement to proof credibility, which facilitates crimes. Buildings are hired in credible locations to receive clients, formidable pictures of lands sale are exposed, as well as network abroad to attest reliability. Individuals or multinationals solicit such services after paying a requested fee for registration. Which further extend to an agreement between a representative of the company or individual usually requiring the name, job description, phone number, resident area and email, for criminal activities which usually take the following patterns; Credit card phishing (online payment), Spyware, Cyber bullying and Identity theft

The call for tenders to award contracts has increased the rate of crimes in developing countries. Social engineering help criminals forged letterhead of state institutions by criminals requesting companies and entrepreneurs to lobby for contracts through defaced websites and spoofed mails. The use of fake documents, security software and virtual accounts is challenging, though some meet client in foreign country 'face-a-face' or in a location where the suppose piece of land is located and make away with the client's money '419'

The Constructive Theory[29]

Agency or Company

- Advertisement of killer post (plot or piece of lands and contracts for construction companies as well as recruitment)
- Registration of guest or customers (fee)
- Information gathering by agency and signature of a contract client before the tour.
- Information then used for phishing, harassment or bullying of the said "customer"

Representative of buyer

- Contact agency with information provided by agent or relative in need of piece of land
- Registration fee for tour
- Sign a contract providing vital information of the representative and the third party to the agency before tour or viewing pictures of the various plots located in strategic areas.

Real buyer

- The person through an online check came across the agency, and in quest for a piece of land for real estate.
- Most of the buyers are usually abroad, seeking to invest home in case of any return or for the future.
- They are prone to cybercrimes, since e-commerce is more advance in the West than in developing countries, most wire huge sum of money to these criminals in the quest for land.

---

29 The constructive theory explains the evolution of cyber criminality in multinational and state contracts. The theory developed after a survey in 2019 in the bid to explain embezzlement and money laundry in state contracts.

In relation to contracts law, the theory demonstrates how senior officials as well as cybercriminals create fictitious companies to be awarded contracts from the government and multinational organizations to share the booty with the company. Renowned companies are vulnerable to such acts by not only cybercriminals but also nationals in states. Where fictitious company are created, contracts awarded to construct, tar roads and construct damns, request retro-commissions[30] from multinational companies or private individuals engaged in the project or contract. Cybercriminals continue to aspire to stage attacks on vulnerable companies, as websites are designed, similar to that of construction companies, requesting for consultants and engineers curriculum vitae, motivation letter and method of salary payment, asked to specify bank, they request for the account number and work tirelessly to breach these accounts.

This theory is relevant to companies and stakeholders that control and ensure the respect of state policy. Companies need to verify offers online and request for information from state or institutions concerning the award of contracts. Also, purchase or payment for real estate online have increased vulnerability rate in the world and particularly in developing countries, because of cybercrime and identity theft. Companies and agencies providing these facilities must be investigated.

Challenges of Criminal Investigations

Case study 1: International Mobile Equipment Identity (IMEI) as a strategic challenge

Criminal investigations are sometimes aborted or closed either for inadequate funds or tracking the wrong person. The prevalence of dark markets in some African countries contributes to cybercriminal escape. Cybercriminals purchase cell phones and laptops, use for a particular period of time and sell in dark market which others purchase. This usually divert criminal profiling and forensic, as law enforcement sturn track an innocent person who

---

30 Retro-commission is a business engagement usually in percentage handed to a state authority after awarding a project to a multinational company.

purchase the phone or laptop at a cheap rate. For formatting a laptop does not prevent it from security investigations, technological advancement; recovery software and forensic investigations.

Also, a terrorist can use a phone and dump; an individual picks and sends to his brother in Africa. When the security agency begins tracking the phone and monitoring the movement of the individual in Africa, locate and apprehend him, they discover the phone was sent or sold to him by a person coming from abroad, not aware it was used by a terrorist.

Case study 2: Subscriber Identity Module (SIM) card registration: An increasing challenge in African

The cheap rate at which SIM cards are sold in some countries without proper security measures is a major justification of the evolution of cyber criminality in some African countries. Mobile operating agencies are out for profit and agents don't usually ensure proper security measures. In an interview with an agent of a mobile operating company agent, she said "if cybercriminals are ahead of law enforcement officers is because sometimes those selling SIM cards register them with their ID cards. This protects the identity of the cybercriminals, as they operate with sim cards registered with the vendors' name. Some vendors also provide or sell codes of the various tariff systems as well as codes of business clients to criminals."

Case study 3: Illegal access

Unauthorized access of electronic communication networks (Wi-Fi) and information system are patterns adopted by cyber criminals. The use of someone's internet network (hot spot, internet sharing with phone and mobile kit) for malicious activities without the knowledge of the person. This incriminates the person's whose phone is used for browsing, when the IP and phone is been tracked by criminal department. For instance, if Baba logs in to a company's VPN, using their connection for malicious activities and the law enforcement officers will be focusing on the wrong target.

More so, the battle between cyber criminals and law enforcement officers expands on data trafficking, IP addresses, to map the specific location of the dons. Data exposes the location, route, time, date, size and duration of the service used. Most crimes are perpetrated in cybercafés to avoid direct traces which most cybercafé operators know little or nothing about these crimes. Identifying cybercafés does not solve the problem, because cybercriminals still exploit Wi-Fi and some criminals are vest with security software.

Furthermore, protecting electronic communication network and information system is a major concern. Following the problem of reliability and durability, the modification and destruction of information strategic elements for criminal investigation and inadequate training of law enforcement officers on cyber security. For instance how would security experts explain why financial transaction carried out by victims cannot be traced in the database system of some banks? This demonstrates staff dishonesty, no collaboration with network service providers, banks and corruption of staff.

Case study 4: Confidentiality

Confidentiality is a serious challenge in matters of security. Maintaining information is one of the major problem in Africa, financial transactions are been phished and unauthorized access and disclosure of information by cyber criminals and hackers. An example is August 2012 Boko-Haram cyber-attack on personal records database of the Nigerian secret service[31]. Cyber criminals have adopted new strategies of getting documents that can secure their identities. They go for attestation of loss of ID card which they use for malicious activities. Now scamming is ancient narrative, but of hacking is the new "game". As convention crimes have taken a different dimension following technological innovation. Criminals gather personal information from social media and also create killer post of American Lottery to grab information of victim, who register on such sites and pay certain fee.

---

31 Ioannis Mantzikos (2013) explains the various challenges faced by security service with the technological revolution with Nigeria cyber-attacks an appeal for other African states.

A Review of Best Practices For Developing Countries

a) The US Strategy

Following the changing patterns of crime and technological evolution in America which has led to cybercrimes as a security threat by individuals like Edward Snowden a former National Security Agency consultant, Julian Assange the founder of wikileaks and groups like "Anonymous" the government of the U.S. has adopted measures to deal with internet crimes through legislation and awareness conferences are organized in order to manage criminal activities. The action has been extended through international and regional collaboration with countries that are willing to participate to share expertise with the U.S.

The United States has taken many measures to combat cybercrime both at the federal and at the state level. There are many state and local law enforcement agencies that are attempting to combat cybercrime within neighborhoods and communities. The United States Secret Service, the Department of Homeland Security, the Federal Bureau of Investigation (FBI) and other state agencies have departments that focus on cybercrimes. These detachments, along with many private establishments collaborate to protect the public and the critical infrastructure of the United States by working to prevent, detect, and stop cybercrimes. Such agencies provide information to the public on how to protect themselves and family from cybercrime. These agencies are organized in such a way that they receive reports or complaints from victims of cybercrimes. These agencies collaborate with other institutions in order to combat the increasing number of cybercrimes. The Department of Homeland Security (DHS) for example has a National Cyber Security Division whose mission is to work collaboratively with public, private and international entities to secure cyberspace and America's cyber assets.

The DHS is focused on protecting not only the government but also individuals from cyber threats (Hacking, Hijacking and DDOS). The DHS Cyber Security Division is structured in three parts: the National Cyberspace Response System, Federal Network Security, and Cyber-risk Management Programs (2011). These separate divisions better enable the DHS to fulfill its goal of protecting cyberspace.

The Department of Homeland Security also operates a Cyber-risk Management Program. In October, the DHS hosts the National Cyber Security Awareness Month, which is designed to educate people about the risks of using the internet (US DHS 2011). They also have a campaign called 'Stop. Think. Connect'. The campaign advises individuals to stop before using the internet and think about the risks present on the internet. People then need to think about their actions on the internet and whether they might be at risk or become victims. The DHS believes that the more knowledgeable someone has about cybercrime, the more he will be able to protect himself.

The FBI focuses on three kinds of cybercrime. First, is a computer intrusion? Computer intrusions includes viruses, spyware, hacking, and other cybercrimes in which the computer is the target (The FBI, 2011). The FBI concentrates on computer intrusions because of the huge financial and security threat posed by these intrusions. Cybercrimes in which the computer is the target poses a threat to national security by rendering critical infrastructure compromised. The financial cost to recovering systems that have been victimized by computer intrusions was evaluated in billions (The FBI, 2011). The FBI combats computer intrusions through special task forces and collaboration with other government and private agencies (FBI 2011). Targets of cyber intrusions can report incidents through the FBI's Internet Crime Complaint Center.

Another focus of the FBI Cybercrime detachment is targeting online child pornography. The FBI runs the Innocent Images National Initiative which is a platform designed to combat the proliferation of child pornography/child sexual exploitation (CP/CSE) facilitated by an online computer (FBI 2011). The FBI recognizes the increasing threats of online child pornography that has caused the expansion of computer and internet practice. The FBI is fighting child pornography through undercover investigation of websites, chat rooms, peer-to-peer networks, and

27

other online locations likely to harbour pedophiles. FBI agents assume fake identities and enter these online locations in a hope to communicate with suspects and gather evidence of illegal activity (FBI 2011). By posing as possible targets, FBI agents hope to identify online raiders before they can harm anyone.

The FBI's third focus is on intellectual property theft. Intellectual property theft is "the illegal possession of copyrighted or patented material, trade secrets, or trademark usually by electronic copying." (Rantala, 2008). Illegal copyright infringement and theft can cause copyright proprietors to lose billions of dollars in lost revenue (The FBI, 2011). Computers have made it easier to evade copyright laws and easier to illegally gain access to trade secrets. The FBI (2011) focused on the theft of trade secrets and infringements on products that can impact consumer's health and safety such as counterfeit aircraft, car, and electronic parts. Fake products can be dangerous to everyone and because these products are often traded across borders, it falls under the Federal government's jurisdiction to investigate. They combat intellectual property theft through targeted operations and collaboration with other government and private agencies (FBI, 2011).

In conclusion, several federal law enforcement agencies are working to combat cybercrimes. And include the Secret Service, the Department of Homeland Security, the Federal Bureau of Investigation, and the Internet Crime Complaint Center whose roles is to provide educational information on their websites on how to protect oneself from online victimization as well as more information on their investigations. The role of the Secret Service concerns the protection of critical infrastructure. This is similar to the situation in Africa where institutions are established to secure state infrastructures like the National Public Key Infrastructure as well as the Computer Incident Response Team (CIRT).

b) Indonesian Strategy

Following the cyber-attacks in Indonesia ranked her as one of the world's top three sources of cybercrime according to Akami Technologies (2013-2014); U.S. based firm in Indonesia. The

Indonesian government structured the fight against cybercrime in five dimensions; technical and procedural measures, legal measures, capacity building, organizational structures and international cooperation (Setiadi et al, 2012).

The Indonesian government has established laws, such as the Telecommunication Act (UU Telekomunikasi No. 36/1999), Information and Electronic Transaction Act (UU ITE No.11/2008) relating to ICT security in Indonesia. The increasing nature of cybercrime in the country led to the Criminal Procedural Law Codex (UU KUHAP), Pornography Act (UU Antipornografi No. 44/2008)[32] and the Copyright Act (UU Hak Cipta No. 19/2002) to combat cyber criminality in Indonesia (Setiadi et al, 2012).

Moreover, there are three government organizations involved in information security in Indonesia. The Information Security Coordination Team, Directorate of Information Security and Indonesia. Security Incident Response Team on Internet Infrastructure (ID-SIRTII). At the technical level, the Indonesian National Standard for Security Management called SNI ISO/ IEC 27001: 2009 for Information Security Management System has strengthened security through briefings. Also, Indonesia is a full member of the Asia Pacific and APCERT FIRST (Forum for Incident Response and Security Team), and the founder of the Organization of the Islamic Conference–CERT (OICCERT) (Setiadi et al, 2012).

In conclusion, the Indonesian government has adopted five measures to fight against cyber criminality. These measures are; the legal measures, capacity building, international cooperation, technical and procedural measures and organizational structures. Most African countries are at the level of capacity building, legal measures and international cooperation, but there is a lack of technical and procedural measures as concerns cyber criminality.

---

32 See; https://www.slideshare.net/SARONMESSEMBEOBIA/understanding-the-new-modus-operandi-of-cybercriminals

c) United Kingdom Strategy

Following the mutations of crime and technological evolution, non-conventional crimes like Cybercrime and Identity Theft has emerged as major security threats as concerns national and international security. The impact on individuals, companies and even national security infrastructures, has made the UK step up legislations and organizations to fight this world's leading security threat. The UK legislators have initiated three acts relating to identity crime; The Forgery and Counterfeiting Act 1981, The Fraud Act 2006 and The Identity Documents Act 2010. The Identity Documents Act 2010 which was formerly the Identity Cards Act 2006 in its section 25(5) & (7) offense for Possessing or controlling a false or illegally obtained ID card which relates to another. The UK also endorsed the Communications Act 2003, the Malicious Communications Act 1988 and in some circumstances the Contempt of Court Act 1981 (Wall, 2013).

Moreover, social networking of children is protected by the UK Council for Child Internet Safety (UKCCIS) was created, to ensure the protection of children online and coordinated by the Department for Children, Schools and Families (DCSF) including the Home Office (Home Office, 2010). Also, the Child Exploitation and Online Protection Centre (CEOP) have developed expertise as a reporting Centre for the public and particularly youths as related to online crimes. The data gathered through reports help identify and create a database for the children involved as well as arrest the perpetrators. The Internet Watch Foundation (IWF) is the UK reporting Centre for websites containing illegal images; it collaborates with law enforcement officers (Wall, 2013).

Furthermore, UK has adopted several approaches through the creation of national agencies to fight against Cybercrime and Identity Theft. The Consumer Direct online reporting Centre and the Fraud Reporting Centre (nFRC), as well as that of CEOP have adopted practical strategies to fight cybercrime and identity theft in the UK. The creation of the National Fraud Authority (NFA) is to collaborate with London Police force against online fraud. The NFA, an executive agency of the Attorney General's Office is the

Government's strategic lead on counter-fraud activity. In 2009, the first National Fraud Strategy was proclaimed (Home Office, 2010). The strategy's four aims are:

1 Creating, collaborating and acting on knowledge

2 Tackling the most serious and harmful threats

3 Apprehend fraudsters to account and reinstate victims,

4 Improve the country's expertise on the fight cybercrime and identity theft.

More so, The Government and the Metropolitan Police Service (MPS) of UK fund the Police Central e-crime Unit (PCeU). The PCeU operates as the central unit for the UK policing on the advancement of standards for training, procedure, and the acknowledgment to e-crime which has brought together forces. The unit also collaborates with City of London Police and Action Fraud to develop responses to electronic fraud reports in connection with the National Fraud Intelligence Bureau (NFIB). The NFRC controls protocols and paves the way for the PCeU in the fight against cybercrime and identity theft. The Serious Organized Crime Agency (SOCA) is an intelligence-led law enforcement agency with major responsibilities to eradicate cybercrime and identity theft (Home Office, 2010).

In conclusion, the United Kingdom (UK) has placed emphasis more on legislation on cybercrime and identity theft than on a practical innovation. The United Kingdom is emerging with new security strategies as concerns cybercrime and identity theft. Cameroon depends on Computer Incident Response Team (CIRT), National Agency for Financial Investigations (ANIF) and International Criminal Police (INTERPOL) branch of Central Africa to fight cybercrimes. Nigeria on her part has the Economic and Financial Crime Commission (EFCC). As such, these government needs to recruit cyber warriors, to crackdown cybercriminals and identity thieves.

Conclusion

Cybercriminals are strategic fellows who exploit security flaws to perpetrate crimes. Though law No. 2010/012 of 21 December 2010 relating to cyber security and cyber criminality in Cameroon has been put in place, the idea or the notion of cyber security as defined by the law remains inactive. Criminals use fake ID cards gotten through social engineering and dishonest staff, due to inadequate collaboration with financial institutions. Security agencies must cooperate with network operators, for profit is the major issues and some turn to neglect the security of other clients. Staff dishonesty exists even within mobile operators and security agencies. As such, those engage in combating this crime should do it with no exemption, because the law is applicable to everyone.

Regarding need for continuous sensitizations on cybercrimes popularly known as "Sakawa" in Ghana, as the government has taken steps to set up cybercrime response teams. The government has set up an emergency cybercrime response team to review actual council, governing the information communication and technology (ICT) activities and strengthen the countries Cyber Security. This effort by the government targets security agencies for capacity building and to enhance the expertise of security agents in identifying the different types of cybercrimes. The action also targets the development of expertise to understand the mutations or changing patterns of crimes to be able to develop a profile of culprits whose innovative criminal skills allow them to employ different tactics and sophistication in carrying out their diabolic and fraudulent transactions. Ghana is classified among the world's top 10 countries in cybercrime.

The preoccupation from cybercrime in Africa particularly in Ghana, led Raymond Code to use the analogy of AIDS to describe the social impact of cybercrime. According to the latter, a legal practitioner's cybercrimes through software computer viruses may in the future mutate data and reconstruct Internet Protocol addresses in the same way that AIDS does to the human body and immune system. The outcome according to the latter would result in emails being misdirected, websites relocated and the internet infrastructure compromised.

Drawing on patterns and the profile of cyber criminals, the situation in Ghana is similar to that in other African countries; victims are vulnerable youths searching for marital relations and get-rich equal schemes. This also includes individuals particularly from rural areas and semi-urban towns ere awareness, and knowledge of information technology is low. As a measure to curs, the activities of fraudsters Jimmy Accotey attached to the said service has called for the confiscation of the property of fraudsters and the strict enforcement of Article 141 of the Electronic Transaction Act 2008. Ghana's effort and increasing search to disrupt, dismantle and prosecute cyber criminals has been championed by the Ministry of Communication on a broad theme titled "ICT4AD - Creating the enabling environment – cybercrime and Laws of Ghana: Strengthening Cyber Security" (GNA).

The Nigerian government has structured the fight against cybercrime and identity theft in three dimensions; technical and procedural measures, legal measures and cyber security cooperation. The Nigerian laws which tackles incidents of cybercrime and identity theft are The Advance Fee Fraud Act of 2006, the Money Laundering Act of 2004 section 12(1) (c) - (d), the Economic and Financial Crime Commission Act of 2005, and the Evidence Act of 1948 as available provisions in the Nigeria criminal law that are used to convict perpetrators of cybercrime (Odumesi, 2014). The Nigeria government has created special security departments to work against cybercrime and identity theft, such as the Economic and Financial Crime Commission (EFCC) which has been providing positive results in the fight against cybercrime with regular raids of public Internet café, arrests and prosecution of suspects. The Nigerian Police Force (NPF) did not report positive results due to lack of adequate Information Technology skills, lack of adequate funding, and lack of necessary motivation to adequately engage cybercriminals[33].

---

33 The cybercrime case that demonstrates the importance of having a law on cyber security and cyber criminality was the case of Akeem Adejumo VS the National Aeronautic and Space Agency of the United States (Odumesi, 2014)

The inadequate knowledge of cybercrime issues and technicalities by Judges in some African states and accumulation of functions is a challenging aspect of criminal investigation[34]. Another challenge is that, sometime electronic evidence tender in several cases to courts are rejected. A typical example that was celebrated is the case of Femi FaniKayode, where the court rejected the printout statement of account because the Evidence Act says you have to produce ledger and right now no banks use ledger anymore (Odumesi, 2014). Law enforcement agencies and cyber security agencies differ in respect to the forensic analysis. Getting evidence to ensure conviction through forensic analysis of suspect's computer systems and devices used to perpetrate the crime demurs a desideratum in Africa and the 'West'.

---

34 National Information Technology Development Agency (NITDA) argued that the major problem towards identifying cybercrime activities is Section 14 of the Nigerian Constitution, which states that "no person shall be punished for a crime unless such crime is prohibited by written law and specific penalties are provided for the violation." As such; the Nigerian Criminal Justice System faced serious challenges with emerging crimes like cybercrime because there was no written law prohibiting any activities on the Internet.

CHAPTER TWO

DEVIANCE IN THE CYBER AGE

Social Media and Deviance

The prevalence of the Internet has presented some unique opportunities for deviant behavior (Rogers, Smoak, & Liu, 2006, p. 246). These opportunities include but not limited to virusware, terrorism, pornography, computer hacking, cyber bullying, and cyber stalking (Giles, 2006; Joinson, 2005). In the same manner, it has also fashioned the modus operandi of existing crimes such as identity theft, cybercrime and money laundering. People have always lied, cheated, and stolen, but the Internet acts as a catalyst of emerging crimes (McDonald, Horstmann, Strom & Pope, 2009, p 2).

With just a click information is gotten, as people participate in group discussions, downloading audio and videos on social networking sites (Adler & Adler, 2008). Individuals easily find others in the cyberspace who share deviant tendencies like pedophiles, lesbianism and homosexuality, and even engage in occult practices through online groups (McDonald, Horstmann, Strom & Pope, 2009, p 2). Jenkins's (2001) "Beyond tolerance: Child pornography on the Internet" articulates better on the contrast of pedophiles experience in the virtual space to that in the real world. For the Internet demure a formidable security threat to fundamentalist tendencies like cyber jihad.

a) Landscape of social media and deviant behavior

Social media is primarily internet or cellular phone based applications and tools use to share data among people, through blogs and forums which allow individuals to interact with one another, often about particular post, news article, pictures or video, and event. (http://www.businessdictionary.com/definition/social-media.html). Miller et al. (2016) observed that, interesting post are flag by people on social networking sites (SNS's) daily. Social media such as Facebook entail that people spend a good deal of time monitoring what others are doing (SCHROEDER, R., 2016). Though considered the leading social networking site, it's not the first to connect the world's population. A survey by Malik, Dhir, and Nieminen (2016) pointed that, photo sharing on Facebook is mainly for an intention to gain popularity and attention or seeking affection and humiliate others. People frequently post photos of social occasions, which include both special events as well as images and videos (nude photos, sex tape and party clips) which affects integrity of others. For photo sharing, Ito and Okabe (2005) speak of "intimate visual copresence," which points toward visual togetherness. But for being together online, photos and videos provide an easier and often richer way of conveying sociability.

b) Cyber Election Interference in U.S

On November 9, 2016 major news networks marked a game over when Donald Trump was shortlisted as the forty-fifth president of the United States of America, following cyber campaign which exposed Clinton's emails she served as U.S. Secretary of State (N.Y. TIMES, Nov. 9, 2016).Clinton's use of a private email server was perceived as a threat to U.S. military machine[1]. The paradox of Trump personal link to the Russian hack into Clinton email servers through public speeches: "Russia, if you're listening, I hope you're able to find the 30,000 emails that are missing," he said, adding "[b]y the way, they hacked—they probably have her 33,000 e-mails. I hope they do. They probably have her 33,000 e-mails that she lost and deleted because you'd see some beauties there (Andy Sherman in Politifact, 2016)[2].

---

1   Patrick Howley, Hillary Clinton Email Scandal Explained, BREITBART (Oct. 31, 2016), http://www.breitbart.com/2016-presidential-race/2016/10/31/hillary-clinton-email-scandal-explained/.

2   https://edition.cnn.com/2016/07/27/politics/donald-trump-vladimir-putin-hack-hillary-clinton

On December 9, 2016, U.S. intelligence officials exposed security challenges, particularly with the confirmation of Russia's involvement in the U.S[3] election. But on June 8, 2017 James Comey testimony pinned Russian in U.S. democracy. "There should be no fuzz on this whatsoever,"[4] Comey stated. "The Russian interfered in our election during the 2016 cycle. They did it with purpose. They did it with sophistication. Yet, consensus built that the Russian interference *did* constitute something that the United States could justifiably call an attack. For Senator Warner: "[A] foreign adversary attacked us right here at home, plain and simple, not by guns or missiles, but by foreign operatives seeking to hijack our most important democratic process—our presidential election."(N.Y. Times, June 8, 2017) and James Comey agreed. "This is such a big deal," he said, because "we have this big, messy, wonderful country where…nobody tells us what to think, what to fight about, what to vote for, except other Americans… But we're talking about a foreign government that, using technical intrusion, lots of other methods, tried to shape the way we think, we vote, we act" (N.Y. Times, June 8, 2017).The Russian interference in U.S. 'game' exposed the 'cyber cold war' in the Western world and particularly super powers. Which some scholars and policymakers alienates to a war narrative. Another incidence is North Korea's efforts to hack and destroy the Sony[5] computer system in order to gain personal retribution for the release of a film offensive to North Korean leaders.

Russian black hat interfered in four major ways: through theft of information, selective dissemination of information, a propaganda campaign, and efforts to hack into voting systems across the country. Analysis exploring why Russia might "hack" the U.S.

---

3   Read; The Law Of Cyber Interference In Elections P.4

4   https://www.reddit.com/r/QuotesPorn/comments/6g2jwu/there_should_be_no_fuzz_on_this_whatsoever_james/

5   Michael Schmitt, International Law and Cyber Attacks: Sony v. North Korea, JUST SECURITY (Dec. 17, 2014), https://www.justsecurity.org/18460/international-humanitarian-law-cyber-attacks-sony-v-north-korea/.

election[6] has focused on Putin's past frustration with U.S. efforts to promote civil society, which president Putin saw as unreasonable intrusion on Russian sovereignty. David Sanger noted in the New York Times, that Putin publicly accused Clinton of instigating protests in Moscow in 2011, and blamed Clinton for encouraging anti-Russian revolts during the 2003 Rose Revolution in Georgia and the 2004 Orange Revolution in Ukraine—each of which Putin saw as unwarranted intrusion into Russia's geographic sphere of influence, rather than as democracy promotion (Eric Lipton et al, 2016).In this manner, Russian interference in the U.S. election can be seen as a tit-for-tat response in guise of President Putin's take (POLITICO MAGAZINE, Dec. 2016).

Russia used various cyberespionage teams to hack into computers and email systems in the 2016 U.S. election. Again, we know that Russian cyber warriors gather data from these computers and systems, because sensitive information and emails it discovered through unauthorized access. A Russian cyberespionage team, colloquially known as "Cozy Bear" or "A.P.T. 29,"[7] hacked computers at the Democratic National Committee (D.N.C) and penetrated the email account of Clinton's presidential campaign chair, John Podesta (Craig Forcese, 2016).Russia also hacked the Republican National Committee (R.N.C) emails using a Russian unit called "Fancy Bear," or "A.P.T. 28."[8] In addition, Russia conducted a massive operation to target hundreds to thousands of non-governmental organizations and non-profits[9].

---

6   https://law.yale.edu/sites/default/files/area/center/global/document/van_de_velde_cyber_interference_in_elections_06.14.2017.pdf

7   David E. Sanger and Scott Shane, Russian Hackers Acted to Aid Trump in Election, U.S. Says, N.Y. TIMES (Dec. 9, 2016), http://www.nytimes.com/2016/12/09/us/obama-russia-election-hack.html?_r=0.

8   David E. Sanger and Scott Shane, Russian Hackers Acted to Aid Trump in Election, U.S. Says, N.Y. TIMES (Dec. 9, 2016), http://www.nytimes.com/2016/12/09/us/obama-russia-election-hack.html?_r=0. The intelligence community's finding is currently, actively, disputed by the R.N.C.; officials argue that Russia never hacked their emails. Id.

9   Full Transcript and Video: James Comey's Testimony on Capitol Hill, N.Y.Times (June 8, 2017), https://www.nytimes.com/2017/06/08/us/politics/senate-hearing-transcript.html?_r=0.23

Second, Russia selectively disseminated some of the hacked emails. Russian intelligence officials took the emails and private documents procured through the hack, and posted them to WikiLeaks and other websites in July 2016[10]. R.N.C. emails, on the other hand, were not disseminated. Russian dissemination of information arguably had significant impact on congressional races, and citizen trust in the democratic process more generally. The fallout from the dissemination of D.N.C. emails was immediate[11]. Debbie Wasserman Schultz, the chair of the D.N.C., was forced to resign, along with her top aides[12]. On the state level, confidential documents taken from the Democratic Congressional Campaign Committee relating to congressional races in a dozen states were published[13], tainting many affected races with accusations of scanda[14].

Third, Russia engaged in "information warfare" campaigns[15]. Sites like RT News and Sputnik, both state-funded Russian sites, shared fake news. Their stories, which attacked Clinton and U.S.-Russian relations, were widely circulated on social media. They were likewise shared by conservative talk-show hosts and activists, "often not knowing the accuracy of the reports (David Sanger, 2016).In addition, the Kremil was identified by U.S. intelligence

---

10 Eric Lipton, David E. Sanger and Scott Shane, The Perfect Weapon: How Russian Cyberpower Invaded the U.S., N.Y. TIMES (Dec. 13, 2016), http://www.nytimes.com/2016/12/13/us/politics/russia-hack-election-dnc.htm

11 In one tweet, Trump quipped: ""The new joke in town is that Russia leaked the disastrous D.N.C. e-mails, which should never have been written (stupid), because Putin likes me." Donald Trump (@realDonaldTrump), TWITTER (July 25, 2016, 4:31 AM), https://twitter.com/realDonaldTrump/status/757538729170964481.

12 Eric Lipton, David E. Sanger and Scott Shane, The Perfect Weapon: How Russian Cyberpower Invaded the U.S., N.Y. TIMES (Dec. 13, 2016), http://www.nytimes.com/2016/12/13/us/politics/russia-hack-election-dnc.html.

13 Ibid 38

14 Ibid

15 David Sanger, U.S. Officials Defend Integrity of Vote, Despite Hacking Fears, N.Y. TIMES (Nov. 25, 2016), http://www.nytimes.com/2016/11/25/us/politics/hacking-russia-election-fears-barack-obama-donaldtrump.html.

agencies as breaching the websites of the boards of elections for Arizona and Illinois[16].

Fourth, Russia allegedly targeted the voter registration systems in over 20 state election systems. Four of the twenty systems were, in fact, breached[17]. Russian electoral interference went far beyond misinformation campaigns, and instead constituted attempts to breach the core systems of American voting apparatus[18]. A classified National Security Agency report, published online by *The Intercept*, states that Russian hackers who were part of the GRU military agency attempted sent spear-phishing emails to over 100 local election officials at VR systems, a Florida-based technology firm that sells equipment and software for voter registration[19].

c) The press as a model of construct and destabilization; The Cameroon example

The liberalization of the press in Cameroon has come under threat because of varying actions for example "Cameroon is one and indivisible": which Cameroon? (Life Time, Vol. 11 No. 00135 Jan 24 2017, p. 1). The question raised by the formal president of the Cameroon Bar Association, barrister Akere Muna led to his interrogation at the State Defense Secretariat (SED)[20], in relation to the Anglophone crisis which began in Cameroon in 2016.

16 Andy Greenburg, Everything We Know About Russian Election-Hacking, Wired (June 9, 2017), https://www.wired.com/story/russia-election-hacking-playbook/.

17 Danielle Kurtzleben, Contrary to Trump's Tweet, Russian Hacking Came Up Before Election (A Lot), NATIONAL PUBLIC RADIO (Dec. 12, 2016), http://www.npr.org/2016/12/12/505261053/13-times-russian-hacking-cameup-in-the-presidential-campaign.

18 Deb Riechmann and Russ Byoum, Report: Russian Hackers Attacked Election Software Supplier, Time (June 5, 2017), http://time.com/4806709/russia-hack-election-donald-trump-nsa-reality-winner/.

19 Andy Greenburg, Everything We Know About Russian Election-Hacking, Wired (June 9, 2017), https://www.wired.com/story/russia-election-hacking-playbook/.

20 Journal du Cameroon in its publication of 24-03-2017 examines the two article that led to barrister Akere Muna's interrogation; the first was "Cameroon is one and indivisible. Which Cameroon?" while the other he pose "change is

Many Cameroonians subscribe to the fact that, the language used to report the crisis in newspapers and social media crafts panic and misunderstanding among the population, and influence different torts. The words used on headlines push some Cameroonians to think that Anglophone Cameroonians hate their Francophone counterparts. On the other hand, Anglophone Cameroonians assume that they are considered by Francophones and even the governments as underdogs, as many refer to them as "Anglo fools" (Camilla A. Tabe and Njofie I. Fieze, 2018).

According to Van Dijk (1988), vocabulary is an element of microstructure in discourse analysis whose meaning is got from the semantic relation between preposition, syntax, and other rhetorical elements such as coherence, quotations, direct and indirect speech. Some vocabulary found on the headlines of both private and state newspapers indicate obligation, and seem to be incompatibly presented. About 140 of this item are noted and Cameroon Tribune carries just 14, while the private print media has 126 as per 2017[21]. These lexes include high sounding verbs, nouns, adjectives and the auxiliary verb "must". The vocabulary of private newspapers is emotionally oriented. Private newspaper headlines use succinct words that produce imagery to address the Anglophone problem. They also use high sounding verbs to demonstrate government imposing attitude to Anglophones. Consider the italicized words in following headlines from the data.

(1) 11 February must hold in the NW, SW regions, govt insists (The sun, No. 0418 Monday, Jan 23, 2017, P.1)

(2) Minesec decrees school resumption...But teachers say no way (Eden, No. 1003 Monday 23 Jan 2017, p. 1)[22]

(3) Social media blamed for misinformation on Anglophone crisis... Gov't begins crackdown; blocks internet (Chronicle, No.475 Jan. 22, 2016, p. 1). The italicized words above from private newspapers seem

---

investable" in the French language daily, Le Jour of December 19, 2016 and January 10,2017.

21 See Camilla A. Tabe and Njofie I. Fieze (2018) P. 10

22 Ibid 46

to portray government's daunting approach to Anglophones during the crisis. Private newspapers equally use nouns, action verbs, and descriptive adjectives to produce some mental pictures about the Crisis. This can be seen in the example below.

(4) Spirit of the struggle lives on, Buea mayor purchases 20 taxis to fight ghost town (The post, No. 01792 Friday, Jan 27, 2017, p.1).

This example indicates that resistance from Anglophones pushes the government to take extra measures. Some of the verbs and nouns used on private newspaper headlines are very pragmatic, metaphorical and symbolic in significance.

(5) When Bamenda Sneezes, The Nation Catches Cold, The People-The Virus (Breaking News No 021, Jan 18, 2017 p. 1)[23].

The headline above is metaphorical because it is used to describe the role played by various actors in the struggle. It presents the government of Cameroon as a weak system or person who can easily contract air born diseases, qualifying Bamenda as a strong disease that needs to be avoided. The two words "sneezes and cold" takes us back to history when the Social Democratic Front (SDF) claiming victory of presidential elections in 1992, thought they were frauded in favour of the CPDM (Tabe & Fieze, 2018). When SDF and its militants stormed the streets of Bamenda to protest, many people were shot to death by military men, properties were destroyed and many injuries recorded. From then, the people of North West are known for a revolutionary spirit. They have been series of tensions and strikes in Bamenda, including the Anglophone crisis that has affected the Cameroon economy. Therefore, Bamenda by this newspaper is a canker warm that needs to be handled with care by the Cameroon government. This is why the conclusion of the quotation calls them "the virus".

---

23 See Camilla Arundie Tabe and Njofie Isaac Fieze; A CRITICAL DISCOURSE ANALYSIS OF NEWSPAPER HEADLINES ON THE ANGLOPHONE CRISIS IN CAMEROON

The French and Danish examples

Source: Dorothy E. Denning

Source: David Rand (2015)

Charlie Hebdo is a French journal reputed for satiric cartoons. Muhammad portrait in the magazine which reflects contemporary journalism, marked with critics, flattery and amusement, initiated deviant behavior by some radicals Muslims. The cartoon paints the virtues circle of Muhammad, though Charlie Hebdo conveys their own values: their categorical rejection of fundamentalist fanaticism and their compassion for its victims. For Rand, those offended by the cartoon of Muhammad are either fundamentalist or suffering from an extremely unhealthy hypersensitivity. The depiction of the 'prophet' Muhammad is blasphemous to Muslims. However, Pierre Bayle (1647-1706) argued that, "Blasphemy is scandalous only in the eyes of one who worships the reality being blasphemed." But the cartoonists of Charlie Hebdo are not Muslims. Thus, this ban, if it exists, would not apply to them. Applying religious rule to persons who are not adherents of that religion is a blatant violation of their freedom of conscience[24].

A similar situation occurred in 2006 when everyone was commenting on the infamous Danish cartoons while most of the media refused to publish them[25]. How can one judge a cartoon without seeing it? In the so-called Muslim world, the situation was even worse. Almost all major media decided not to publish the portrait, thus depriving hundreds of millions of readers of essential information, while religious authorities declared the images blasphemous. Once again, the public is instructed on what to think but denied access to the means to inform themselves directly. We need not be astonished that many obeyed and, out of a sense of religious obligation, declare themselves to be duly "offended."[26] This reeks of manipulation, using religion as a tool for political purposes. One is reminded of the controversy surrounding the Danish cartoons, when it was revealed that new intentionally provocative cartoons had been added to the collection by Muslims in order to stir up hatred against the cartoonists[27].

d) Cyber deviance in the music industry

The globalization era has increased the level of social deviance in Africa. Youths in the music industry, have adopted the Western culture of clash and freestyle, creation of groups or gangs and beef amongst adolescents. Drawing from activities in the American music industry, most young Africans engage in drugs abuse

---

24 Jihad and Just War: A Religious Game by Saron Messembe Obia

25 Dorothy E. Denning; The Jihadi Cyberterror Threat, slide 38 http://www.nps. navy.mil/da/faculty/DorothyDenning/index.htm dedennin@nps.edu24

26 Ibid 49

27 Ibid

because of video clips the watch, some create gangs or groups which compete online through social networking channels, as well as insult and attack others through short videos. Social networking channels are increasing becoming a social war, where musician seek to showcase their wealth, talent and costume by insulting fellow musicians.

Music about the marginalization and insecurity in Cameroon

Drawing from Donatus Fai Tangem's, 'Oral history, Collective Memory and Socio-Political Criticism: A study of Popular Culture in Cameroon', it is easy to underscore how popular musical productions evolved from Nkotti François and the Black Style group to Lapiro de Mbanga and Longué Longué. While the thematic slant of the pre-Biya productions were more social and moral, post-Ahidjo musical productions Socio-political problems such as corruption, dictatorship and political discrimination (Fai Tangem, 2016). Nico Mbarga, the Nigerian Cameroonian tracks such as Happy Birth Day and Sweet Mother quickly gave way to the likes of Awilo de Bamenda in Country Don Spoil (2006) and Lapiro de Mbanga's Constitution Constipé (2011). Young revolutionary voices like Saint Bruno in Changement (2001), General Valsero in Lettre au President (2008) and Dynastie le Tigre ft Kedjevara in Pain Sardine (2018) are critical to the ruling elite as well as the socio-political evolution of Cameroon.

Gradually, folk as well as modern musician occupied the center stage seeking an opportunity either for image cleansing or for the popularization of their commercial products. Through the avenue of popular culture, therefore, every social class sought and obtained representations in a medium that cuts across society with its double edges. Antonio Gramsci in Selection from Cultural Writings argues that "When the politician puts pressure on the art of his time to express a particular cultural world, his activity is one of politics not of artistic criticism. If the cultural world for which one is fighting is a living necessary fact, its expansiveness will be irresistible and it will find its artists".

45

The double standard of popular culture or its dynamic operational context, is perceptible where, while one production lambastes either the regime or an individual, the other glorifies the state or the same individual criticized by another production. This is clearly the case of Ngalle Joyo, in his 1993 album Rigueur, who hails and praises the Biya regime, while Benji Mateke, like Prince Yerima Afo Akom decries the misery and frustration caused by the same regime. As if to explain the raison d'etre of artistic activism, Leon Trotsky says, "Generally speaking, art is an expression of man's need for a harmonious and complete life, that is to say, his need for those major benefits of which a society of classes has deprived him. That is why a protest against reality, either it is conscious or unconscious, active or passive, optimistic or pessimistic, always forms part of a really creative piece of work". Apart from the need to redress or even merely spotlight issues in society, what continues to be incontestably true about the artists however is that their products maintain the fundamental functions of oral history as well as the recapitulation of collective memory on one hand, and a cry of despair and socio-political lampoon on other? It is difficult to contemplate a world without music, rhythms for dance and pleasurable distraction.

However, music lends itself to diverse message embodiment and communication and may influence its consumer's behaviour. Thus, music could be used by political and social movements to achieve particular goals. For example Bob Marley and Fela Anikulapo Kuti became legends because of their political conscience music – music that attacked government or the highly placed in society who oppressed or ignored the masses. All forms of violence are manifested or song about in youth music. Some artistes have used their songs to draw attention to social ills in society, particularly structural violence. African China is credited with bringing to public consciousness youth's awareness of, and concern about corruption in government, poor provision of social amenities, maltreatment of the poor, and voice of the voiceless following preferential treatment for the rich. African China and Timaya's choice of word in some of the lyrics are reminiscent to a purists view of the world (Christopher, 2013).

Fraud, corruption and cybercrime sung about and portrayed in music videos show how to make quick and easy money. Christopher Nkechi in his work observed that, *Yahoozee* (by Olu Maintain), gives a vivid picture of what is gained through cybercrime, increased the incidence of cybercrime. The lyrical compass 'If I hammer, first thing *na* Hummer (jeep)' meaning: If I make a hit, the first thing I will buy is a Hummer jeep, made youth crazy about getting money by any means. Similarly, other lines in *Yahoozee* support indolence among youth, suggesting that some are born to harvest the labour of others for revelry.

Internet fraud is gradually becoming a social norm as young musical pundit, promote such in their music. Kelly Hansome's *Maga don pay* [the fraud victim has paid] is explicit in its message on how patience on the Internet by the criminal would yield wealth (Christopher, 2013). The messages in these song lyrics contradict youth musicians' criticism of corruption and other social vices that are associated with structural violence. Some artistes actually promote aggression and enmity in their music. Eedris Abdulkareem satirizes Olusegun Obasanjo and Tuface in *Ko le ye won*, blaming the former president for giving Tuface an award that he (Abdulkareem) deserved. Media effect of youth music may be contestable, but there is no doubt that music consumption elicits youth deviance.

e) Sexual Deviance on Social media

The youths represent majority of the world population (Omolo, 2014). This young population is prone to social networking sites. According to Todd (2009) the youths are exposed to videos, shows, advertisements, and movies with sexual content. In terms of body image, the social media floods the young girls'' minds with images of skinny models[28]. This makes them feel that if they are a few pounds heavier than these images on the websites, then

---

28 Laws & O' Donohue (1997) argued that sexual deviance refers to the nature of sexual behavior that is nonconforming with societal norms or expectations, is of maladaptive nature and interferes with the individual's functioning in Roland Paulauskas (2013) .

they are unacceptable to the society. The proliferation[29] of social networking sites (particularly dating, pedophiles, lesbian and gay) have also increased in recent years, following the large segments of the population in the Western world (Dohring, 2009, p. 1089). Which attest the impact of the Internet on the film industry in relation to pornography.

In Quinn and Forsyth's (2005) sexual behavior in the era of the internet: A typology for empirical research revealed; internet pornography is a $3 billion industry, with about 4.5 million Web sites containing pornographic content, encompassing 25% of total search engine requests, and with more than 75 million people accessing pornographic sites. As online pornography have been associated to unhappy marriages and religious order among adults (Stack, Wasserman, & Kern, 2004), social constraint in families and society among adolescents (Mesch, 2009). King and Stones (2013) posited that the nudity 17 and sharing of pornographic material has been on the rise in Australian schools as a result of the availability of social media channels that young adults are exposed to. This include some causal relationship between online activity and deviant behavior among persons who had not engaged in these behaviors before (nude photos, "virtual" rape or snuff sites, hate behaviors, sex tape for homosexuals, pedophilia and tattoos).

Environmental, social, and psychological characteristics are risk factors associated with online offenders. From Gottfredson and Hirschi (1990) general theory of crimes, ethical consideration is not an exception to the growing vulnerability of the population, due to opportunity or suitable victim and low self-control. Durkin, K., Forsyth, C. J., & Quinn, J. F. (2006), subscribes to Goffman's (1963) analogy on stigma to draw parallels between the Internet and what he described as "back places," or places where people are open to certain tendencies or behaviors[30].

---

29 Rege, A. (2009) explains the emergence of non-conventional crimes with the increasing rate of social networking sites (online dating) linked to new forms of crimes.

30 Halverson, Jeffry, and Amy Way. "The Curious Case of Colleen LaRose: Social Margins, New Media, and Online Radicalization." Media, War & Conflict, 5.2 (2012): 139-153

In Nigeria sexual immorality is highly mention in students 'essays as a predominant form of violence, either on the psyche of the audience or directly on participation in artistic events, which victims are women (Christopher, 2013). Starting from indecent costumes, students listed as forms of violence to women: negative portrayal of women, pornography, use of vulgar language, provocative dance steps, promotion of sex[31] and lust, and the presentation of rape and violent sex as normal and acceptable practices. It is clear that students oppose the demeaning of women in society; that is, they are against misogyny. Abdulkareem had won people's admiration when he condemned lecturers that sexually exploit female students[32], but he also contributes to the genre celebrating sexual immorality (Christopher, 2013). His use of foul language in *Oko Asewo* [the husband of prostitutes] promotes promiscuity in the mind of the simple, to the effect that rape can easily be perpetrated with impunity. Music videos portray women as sex commodities and property for a male to possess, manipulate and discard as deemed fit. An example is D'Banj who unconscionably sings about sex and promiscuity.

f) Cyberbullying on social media

The freshman suicide at Rutgers University due to a Twitter message that made a private moment public exposed the effects of cyberbullying on adolescents (Foderaro, 2010). Cyberbullying is described as a malicious act that may occur over various communication modes including phone, text messaging, e-mails, pictures or video clips, instant messaging, websites, and chat rooms (Smith et al., 2008). The main attributes of cyberbullying include aggression, intention, repetition and power imbalance (Dooley, Pyżalski & Cross, 2009; Kernaghan & Elwood, 2013). The Pew Research Center states that 39 percent of SNS users are likely to experience some form of cyberbullying (Skye, 2012). Picture or video clip bullying in social networking sites (SNSs) have the

---

31 Weitzer, R. (2011) Legalizing Prostitution. From Illicit Vice to Lawful Business

32 Pondi, E. (2011) condemned the deviance behavior amongst students and lecturers in university campuses in Cameroon focusing on the high rate of prostitution and sexual harassment in such milieus.

largest negative impact (Smith et al., 2008). The typical features of social media such as "friends," "comments" and "photos" make SNSs suitable platforms for the display of aggressive and/or offensive behaviors toward another individual or user (Boyd & Ellison, 2007).

1- The case of Colleen LaRose (Jihad Jane)

The globalization period changed the patterns of crimes in the world, from human security threats to the game of nuclear material. Social media is an active factor of post 9/11 international security, following radicalization through social networking sites (SNS's). Colleen LaRose, popularly known as "Jihad Jane," was embraced through a new community (through SNS's) after things fell apart in her marriage (Reyes, 2016). From her marital history, she was exposed to petty crimes like writing bad checks at the age 16 years. LaRose's emotional state and new online community radicalized her, having a different narrative about the world and how it ought to be. Her search over social media, linked her to some individuals that believed to be marginalize and shared a common ideology 'jihad'. Trauma, inadequate rehabilitation, torture and available connection with violent extremists were major factors for her engagement in 'holy war'.

Furthermore, digital content posted on SNSs on a single click are widely disseminated. Just posting an insulting comment or a compromising picture may result in continued and repeated humiliation for the victim (Kernaghan & Elwood, 2013). The ability to connect to a large audience in a short period of time makes SNS cyberbullying a severe form of aggression compared to traditional bullying (Sticca & Perren, 2013). For cyberbullying may begin as early as elementary school, reach the highest level during middle school years, and slightly decrease in high school (Rivituso, 2012).

2- The freshman suicide at Rutgers University

Suicide is increasingly gaming the society, particularly with youths engaged in anti-social behaviors like cyberbullying and breach of privacy. Popularly known as the freshman suicide case at Rutgers

University, the death of Tyler Clementi sparked remorse on teenage attitude in academic milieu, in relation one's sexual alienation. Who wished they could have stopped the teen from jumping off a bridge last week after a recording of him having a sexual encounter with a man was broadcast online. Tyler Clementi, 18, jumped off the George Washington Bridge into the Hudson River. After the discovery of his mortal remains, some controversial arguments made headlines;" Had he been in bed with a woman, this would not have happened," said Lauren Felton, 21, of Warren.

One of the major pattern of young hackers is the use of videos and voice calls to blackmail victims. Ed Schmiedecke, a retired music director at Ridgewood High School, from which Clementi graduated this year, attest he was a great violinist whose life revolved around music. "He wouldn't have been outed via an online broadcast and his privacy would have been respected and he might still have his life."

Clementi's roommate, Dhraun Ravi, and fellow Rutgers freshman Molly Wei, both 18, have been charged for breach of privacy. Middlesex County prosecutors say the pair used a webcam to transmit a live image of Clementi having sex on Sept. 19 and that Ravi tried to webcast a second encounter on Sept. 21, the day before Clementi's suicide.

ABC News and The Star-Ledger of Newark reported on Clementi's Facebook post on Sept. 22 which read: "Jumping off the gw bridge sorry." On Wednesday, his Facebook page was accessible only to friends. Several gay rights groups linked Clementi's death to the troubling phenomenon of young people committing suicide after being harassed over their sexuality. Nine out of 10 gay, lesbian and bisexual students are bullied in school, according to a 2007 survey by the Gay, Lesbian and Straight Education Network, CBS News National Correspondent Jeff Glor reported on "The Early Show" Thursday. They are four times more likely to attempt suicide, according to a 2007 Massachusetts youth risk survey.

An epistolary written by Richard McCormick, Rutgers University President to the campus read, "If the charges are true, these actions gravely violate the university's standards of decency and humanity." The university on Wednesday was launching a two-year Project Civility, designed to get students thinking about how they treat others (The New York Time, 2011). The Clementi's case gave a different narrative about youths interaction in the academic milieu, the emergence of cyberbullying and gender discrimination (The New York Time, 2011). Mr. Ravi, of Plainsboro, N.J., is charged with multiple counts of invasion of privacy, trying to deceive investigators and intimidation as a bias crime, based on Mr. Clementi's sexual orientation. The papers that Mr. Ravi's lawyer, Steven D. Altman, included with his motion do not paint an entirely flattering picture of his client.

The Former Rutgers Student Faces up to 10 Years in Prison and Deportation to India. Ravi's freshman roommate Tyler Clementi committed suicide days later. "I do not believe he hated Tyler Clementi," Judge Glenn Berman told the court. "He had no reason to, but I do believe he acted out of colossal insensitivity." (Koenigs, Smith and Christina NG, 2012) Rutgers Trial: Dharun Ravi Sentenced to 30 Days in Jail. Ravi, 20, must report to Middlesex Adult Correctional Center on May 31 at 9 a.m. for his 30-day jail term. He was also sentenced to three years' probation, ordered to complete 300 hours of community service and attend counseling programs for cyber-bullying and alternative lifestyles.

He must also pay a $10,000 assessment to the probation department in increments of $300 per month beginning Aug 1. The money will go to victims of bias crimes. The judge recommended that Ravi, who was born in India and is here on a green card, not be deported. "I heard this jury say, 'guilty' 288 times--24 questions, 12 jurors. That's the multiplication," Berman said. "I haven't heard you apologize once." Ravi was convicted of invasion of privacy, bias intimidation, witness tampering and hindering arrest, stemming from his role in activating the webcam to peek at Clementi's date with a man in the dorm room on Sept. 19, 2010. Ravi was also convicted of encouraging others to spy during a second date, on Sept. 21, 2010, and intimidating Clementi for being gay.

Theoretical analysis of the freshman suicide case

Neutralization Theory

Neutralization theory focuses on community policing, that both law-abiding individuals and lawbreakers, but delinquency results from an unconscious defense of deviant behavior (Sykes & Matza, 1957). Is a model use for the jusytification of deviant behavior for criminals in order to validate antisocial behaviors. These justifications are known as neutralization techniques.

Sykes & Matza (1957) articulated on five neutralization techniques to be used to justify antisocial behavior; denial of responsibility, denial of injury, denial of the victim, condemnation of the condemners, and appeal to higher loyalties. We suggest that denial, rather than naiveté, is involved in cyberbullying because educational initiatives in public school systems often include presentations to warn students about inappropriate online behavior such as cyberbullying (Ahmed, Harris, & Braithwaite, 2006). Public media has also warned society about the negative consequences of cyberbullying (Dooley et al., 2009). The attention to cyberbullying in schools due to the awareness of adolescents about the potential for social media to be used as a cyberbullying tool.

Consequently, the use of SNSs to cyberbully is unlikely to be inadvertent, but rather an intentional act. Since cyberbullying is not a face- to-face behavior, perpetrators can avoid seeing the victims' pain and emotional distress (Cassidy, Faucher & Jackson, 2013).

Additionally, cyberbullies may treat the asynchronous communication of SNSs as an escape route if they feel they can distance themselves from the harmful information. For example, a synchrony may contribute to denial if it enables the cyberbully to avoid responsibility, "It feels safe putting the message out there where it can be left behind" (Suler, 2004, pp. 323). Thus, in accordance with neutralization theory, a cyberbully is likely to understand what constitutes cyberbullying behavior but may defend his/her actions based on denials that arise from the ability to distance himself from the encounter via the characteristics of SNSs, such as a synchronicity.

g) Denial of Responsibility

There is always a tendency for criminals to refute their crimes, and relating it to societal factors. According to the denial of responsibility neutralization technique, the delinquent shifts accountability for a deviant behavior to another party by claiming that the environment or outside factors are responsible for his behavior (Sykes & Matza, 1957). Research indicates that perpetrators and bystanders are more likely to attribute the responsibility for cyberbullying to the victim when the victim appears to be extroverted and willingly discloses personal information online (Weber, Ziegele & Schnauber, 2013). Some cases where suspects endorse an act, torts about society is changed and he turns to perform good deeds (Morrison, 2006). In contrast, when individuals shifted the responsibility for their cyberbullying, they were more likely to continue to cyberbully. We surmise that a SNS cyberbully who shifts the responsibility for his actions by blaming others or environmental circumstances is using the denial of responsibility technique to rationalize his offenses. This neutralization technique relieves the perpetrator of personal culpability and may allow offensive behavior to continue or escalate.

h) Sanctions and Severity of Sanctions

Facebook as case study

policing white collar crimes and implementing sanctions on those engaged in such on different social networking sites is usually essential. Sanctions represent disincentives and in the context of cyberbullying the construct is comprised of formal sanctions, informal sanctions and shame. Formal sanctions are the implementation of stated consequences that would result from cyberbullying behavior. It is typical for SNSs to post policies stating objectionable behaviors as well as consequences for performing those behaviors. Posted policies and user guidelines are often conditions with which the user must 'agree' before activating the site. For example, in the "Statement of Rights and Responsibilities" of Facebook (2012), the consequences of cyberbullying in Facebook are described as "disable your account," "stop providing all of Facebook to you," and "stop providing part of Facebook to you." It is expected that these formal sanctions would activate cost or benefit considerations (Blumstein et al., 1978) in the decision to engage in cyberbullying and serve as a disincentive.

Informal sanctions are potential costs or risks that may not be explicitly stated or policy-driven, but nevertheless may result from the commission of a deviant act. Informal sanctions may include job loss, social and personal embarrassment or the disapproval of friends or family (Paternoster & Simpson, 1996). Facebook users connect with 'friends' and family members in different communities. Thus, informal sanctions are related to the loss of respect from one's friends, family members and/or communities when they become aware of one's cyberbullying behavior.

Drawing from analysis of the theory of deterrence and rational choice support the argument that one will often choose to act in one's own self-interest when weighing benefits and risks, as cyberbullying may result to media attention when the consequences are tragic or may be shared within SNS communities, the risk of others knowing of one's behavior serves as an informal deterrent (Cassidy et al., 2013).

The third facet of sanctions is shame. Shame is depicted as an emotional state or condition characterized by embarrassment, dishonor, disgrace and humiliation (Broucek, 1991). While shame may be considered a type of informal sanction, it has been conceptually differentiated from informal sanctions because of its self-imposing nature (Paternoster & Simpson 1996). Whereas informal sanctions originate from what others think and may result in the loss of respect for a cyberbully, shame is self-inflicted and originates within the one who victimizes others. Thus, shame is a separate and independent dimension of sanctions. Traditionally, shame has been an effective deterrent of antisocial behaviors and thus is expected to operate as an important facet of sanctions. Shame may be managed by the individual in two ways: shame acceptance and denied responsibility (Morrison,

55

2006). acknowledgement tended to deter bullying while shame displacement predicted bullying (Ahmed et al., 2006)[33].

Conclusion

According Stern and Handel (2001), although the Internet is relatively new, its power and ability are influential on social values. Social media demure a formidable threat to human security (through its multiple channels used for extremism and religious fundamentalist ideas by some individuals) and deviant behaviour (cyberbullying, pornography and gangster life, just to name a few). Patricia and Ndung'u (2014) and Omolo (2014) have the same narrative on anti-social behavior to social media, drawing from the case of Karen and Runda youths respectively (they engage in drugs abuse and sexual orgies). The negative influence of social media on youths is due to the proliferation of digital devices (smart phones) which ease access to sexual channels on the internet (Kiragu, 2015).

Education is a major skill for the acquisition of a job because it provides the prerequisite and specific qualities that satisfy the quality and security of a job. This requirement is very influential regarding the level of recruitment in most African countries (Akuta et al: 2011). There is inefficiency in criminal investigation due to low level of education. This is a constraint in apprehending cybercriminals who in some cases are graduates[34] with, certificates from universities in the country. Teenagers are equally covered by the privacy rule provide by some social networking sites, contributing to the sharing of explicit content. Cyber criminality demands a given level of awareness and knowledge of information technology, economics and commerce as well as a certain degree of exposure and intellectual ability (Aluko 2004).

---

33 Shame is a psychological trait when a bad behavior is acknowledged and responsibility asserted, which is a deterrent factor for social construct.

34 See; ScamWarners.COM or ScamSurvivors.COM

CHAPTER THREE

BIOMETRIC SYSTEM AND DIGITAL FORENSICS

Forensic comes from the Latin word 'forensis'[1], in the domain of criminology, forensic science applies to courts or the judicial system. Forensic science is the combination of methods and processes in solving crimes (that is to uncover mysteries and convict or exonerate suspects of crimes). Forensic experts use complex gadgets or tools, scientific principles and reference precedents to analyze evidence as to identify certain criminal patterns. Digital forensics is the process of uncovering and interpreting electronic data[2]. The aim of the process is to preserve any grounded evidence while performing structured investigation by gathering, identifying and validating the information in order to reconstitute past events[3]. A biometric system is a technological system that uses data about a person to identify that individual. Biometric systems recaptures specific data about unique biological traits in order to work effectively[4].

Several factors are to be considered when designing a multi-modal biometric system. The choice and number of biometric systems selected, is largely driven by the nature of the system and the organizations requirements.

---

1   See;crimesceneinvestigationedu.org

2   https://www.bartleby.com/essay/Digital-Forensics-Is-The-Process-Of-Un-covering-F3XWCF5ZLJXQ

3   See;https://www.techopedia.com.definition

4   Ibid

This includes considerations like the accuracy of the trait; the matching operation; the population; the memory demands of the algorithms; and the security of multiple devices. Biometrics are based on the measurement of distinctive physiological or behavioural characteristics. Fingerprint, face, iris, hand, and retina are considered physical, or physiological, biometrics, as they are based on direct measurements from parts of the human body. This also incorporates user behaviour, or the manner in which a person presents a finger, or looks at a camera. Therefore, physical biometrics directly measure characteristics of the human body. Digital forensic is the procedure of investigating non-conventional crimes (Farhood N. Dezfoli et al, 2013)[5].

Smart phone has easy access to a camera and voice recorder, so a combination of face and voice biometrics, might be more appropriate. So in biometric implementation, simplicity is what we should be aiming for. Simplicity comes from a combination of clarity of purpose and good system design. Within such a model, the systems architecture should be sufficiently able to support the operational and processing requirements with no unnecessary links to other systems. Another challenge that is becoming more and more prevalent is identity theft. Due to loopholes in both government and commercial processes, it is relatively easy to gather a good deal of information about a targeted individual. Obtaining a single relevant reference can often be enough to effectively steal someone's identity and use it for fraudulent purposes. In such cases, it is often extremely difficult for the true holder of the identity to reject the fraudulent usage and re-establish their good credentials. The more extensive the collecting and storing of an individual's personal information, the higher the risk.

---

5   Many research have been carried out on forensic investigation and its challenges. As such, biometric system will depend on data available, necessary for criminal investigation following forensic patterns. For instance an National ID Scheme for a large country like Nigeria may require both Irises and Fingerprint enrolment, for citizen identification, due to its population and need to match in criminal database.

Biometric Classification

On the other hand, voice recognition, gait, and signatures are considered behavioural biometrics, as they are based on measurements and data derived from an action and human body composition, such as the shape of the vocal cords in a voice scan, or the agility of hands and fingers in signature recognition. Therefore, behavioural biometrics measures these human body characteristics indirectly.

Physiological and behavioural classifications are a useful way to view the different types of biometric technology traits. However, both classifications have performance and privacy-related issues depending on which modality is being implemented. The problem of authentication and identification is always very challenging, and establishing the identity of an individual is a complex puzzle.

Current approaches in solving the problem of authentication and individual identity can be considered in two ways:

Identity or datamining; For example, you can permit physical access to a building to all individuals whose identity is authenticated by giving them a key; and a person's knowledge of a piece of information. An individual can gain access to a computer system if they know the user-id and password associated with it. (Jain, 2015) When you conduct an EFTPOS transaction, you are using both datamining or confidential information (your Bank or Credit Card), and (your pin number) to identify yourself. However, these approaches can be exploited, with the card stolen or lost, the pin number forgotten or shared. The problem with this is, that once you have lost control of your identifying possession, such as the PIN number, then an unauthorised person can use your possession for fraudulent activities. While biometric technologies are not the magic bullet in solving identification, when they are combined with the other methods of proof, these technologies are beginning to provide very powerful tools for solving positive identification problems and identify theft.

Biometric Patterns For Organizations

Biometric technologies are used for many simple applications in business; such as time and attendance of employees for a small business, to the security and confidentiality of a 23 million democratic voting process for a large business.

Depending on the application, the benefits of using biometrics are: increased security and reducing fraud attempts, as well as improving services and convenience for clients. Therefore, in some applications, the biometric may only serve as a deterrent, however, in others, it is central to system security.

Biometric applications can be categorized into three main groups:

- Commercial applications; such as physical access control, logical access, and Internet banking.

- Government applications; such as national identity cards, social security payments, and border security.

- Forensic applications; such as law enforcement, criminal identification, and disaster victim identification.

Commercial applications of biometrics, as they not only secure and improve existing financial services, but also enable secure remote services to be offered that would not be otherwise possible without biometrics.

Access control systems use biometrics to identify or verify the identity of persons entering or leaving an area, typically a room or building. This is the biometric used to complement or replace antiquated mechanisms such as keys, tokens, passes and badges. These systems are usually adopted to allow access to selected rooms in a facility, building, or office environment, and are rarely used to control access to every door. Access control is also critical to financial institutions, especially those with on-site vaults, safety deposit boxes, and other areas in need of security. The core benefit for the customer is bank security.

However, it has the added advantage that it allows for customers to access their safety deposit boxes without needing to wait for assistance from a bank staff member. In some countries, banks control access to safe deposit boxes using facial-scan technology. Biometric technologies can also be used to identify or verify the identity of individuals conducting transactions on ATMs. Biometric authentication for access control is a highly compelling solution, as keys and badges are easily shared without being traceable back to the actual user, whereas biometrics cannot be shared.

E-commerce, or Internet banking, is seen as a desirable area for biometrics to enable the identification and verification of individuals conducting remote transactions for goods and services. These applications of biometric technologies are used to complement or replace other authentication mechanisms such as passwords, PINs, and secret questions. There is no biometric infrastructure to leverage from, any implementation of biometrics would require that the financial institution supply readers to customers, and the current PIN and password model involved in online account access operations work well enough that institutions have not rushed to replace it. However, some banking institutions are already piggy-backing on biometric phone technologies in order to offer biometric access to online banking.

Biometric Strategy For States

Citizen identification are necessary for state institutions to easily identify or verify individuals interacting with government agencies for the purposes of card issuance, voting, immigration, social services, or employment background checks.

Biometrics are used to complement or replace current authentication methods, such as document provision, signatures, or vouchers; and provide unique functionality if it is used to prevent duplicate registration for a public benefit or service. Biometric technologies are increasingly being used to authenticate and identify individuals at national or state borders. Some countries in conjunction with others conduct several pilot programs testing the feasibility of biometric deployments across borders, particularly with the problem of illegal immigrants and unauthorised foreign workers entering country each day.

The Australian Taxation Office uses "voiceprint", a voices can biometric system, to verify voice matches against tax file numbers. As the ATO receives over 6 million callers each year it is hoped that this will improve the time it currently takes to perform identification checks. eGate systems continue to increase in popularity as a way of expediting the processing of travelers across International airports – Australia and New Zealand are adopting face recognition technologies, Vancouver and Chicago have integrated fingerprint technologies, and Dubai will capture both facial and retinal scans to establish the individual's identity.

An e-passport is a biometric passport that offers improved security with an embedded microprocessor chip. This contains all the data required to authenticate an international traveler and is often used in association with eGate. The data stored on the chip uses PKI, or Public Key Infrastructure, to protect and ensure information has been authenticated by an authorized organisation and that the digital signature meets the standards set by the International Civil Aviation Organisation (ICAO), which is an agency overseen by the United Nations. Match the iris to the owner's eye.

Additional security features have also been added to e-passports, such as Basic Access Control which prevents the chip from being wirelessly read by unauthorised organisations, and Active Authentication which offers further security and protection of personal information stored on the chip. National Identification cards have digitally embedded biometric information which is used to effectively control the collection of social security benefits, minimise identify theft, and manage immigration on a very large scale.

In many countries, the driver's license is also used as an identification document, therefore it is important to prevent the duplication of multiple drivers' licenses. With the use of biometrics, this problem can be eliminated. However, it is important that the data must be shared between states and territories because in some countries the licenses are controlled at the state level as opposed to the federal level.

Forensics Investigation And Biometrics

Tracking And Identifying Criminals

People take advantage of the anonymity of the Internet to facilitate electronic crimes. Abuse of the anonymity of Internet by criminals is a predictable but inevitable dark side in an information society. The difficulty of tracing and identifying criminals is one of the main hurdles that cyber investigators meet every day. On the other hand, techniques used for tracing criminals can be applied to locating non-cybercriminals as well. The Korean Police has been making efforts to develop tracing techniques and the products are being widely used for every kind of criminal investigation.

Tracing is rarely confined to a single action, but rather a series of tedious operations. It is not odd if an investigator sends dozens of written requests seeking legal permission from prosecutors and courts in an investigation. To minimize the burden, investigation should be planned strategically and tactically. In many cases, critical information can be provided by service providers, including Internet Service Providers (ISP). Needless to say, maintaining intimate relationships is important. Unfortunately, getting helpful information from service providers is frequently difficult for many reasons. An investigator needs technical or human skills to overcome such difficulty. Experienced investigators in the CTRC who know the possibility and the limitation of each technique are available to answer questions concerning tracing matters.

Basic Communication Information given by Service Providers

Communication is a strategic tool in criminal investigation and acquiring data for legal procedures is usually tedious. It usually takes more than a day to complete the whole process unless there is an emergency situation. That is why time management is important. Otherwise, cybercrime investigation will be a chain of requests for communication information with a risk of the case failing. Service providers should make available a list of identified persons and sim cards sold on the street to police department to help combat cybercrimes. They should also implement a real-time notification scheme via an investigator's mobile phone or closed webpage to provide the information possibly containing the cell location of a mobile phone, log-on and log-off status and IP address.

Internet Cafés

Cybercriminals, 419ners or Ngues Men usually like operating in internet cafes or cyber cafes. Once the target of a trace action can be identified by an online user account or nickname, there is a possibility to capture the suspect before he or she leaves the Internet café. The Korean National Police approach can be adopted by Sub-Saharan African countries to combat the emergence of cyber criminality. Where the entire country and a dispatch system using police radio make it possible for the responders, typically patrol officers, to reach any Internet Café within 10 to 15 minutes. There have been several arrest like a bank robber who gambled online in an Internet café after committing the robbery. Investigators find out other clues through forensics investigation. Cyber investigators sometimes forget the importance and potential of physical traces such as hair, print and fiber may have to be collected for further investigation. Investigators also have to be cautious cyber cafes management in the recovery of criminal data, particularly PCs in Internet cafés hardware or software-based hard disk recovery tools requiring more careful treatment.

IP Laundry

Criminals want to be shielded behind computers to block tracing back by investigators. Since a computer is identified by an IP address, blocking is often called IP laundry. IP laundry is more common for average criminals and this is a universal problem in law enforcement. There is no perfect criminal haven, but, depending on the technique used for IP laundry, some tracing methods are extremely difficult to adopt and very time-consuming. Basic IP laundry techniques are categorized as follows ;

> IP concealing: Hides the existence of original systems used by a perpetrator by a detour using an intermediate system through a specific Internet service such as proxy, secure shell, socks, VPN, remote control, and so on;

> IP forgery: Changes source IP address in packets to conceal and deceive origin. Address Resolution Protocol (ARP) spoofing is usually implemented to intercept communications, called sniffing, but also can be used to hide origin;

> Domain Name System (DNS) altering: Does not conceal or change IP addresses of the source computers. Instead, it often changes the source computers themselves, typically zombies, by the using of the functionality of dynamic DNS.

Techniques to defeat IP laundry vary are not limited to these methods;

Tracing Method for Individual Internet Services

> E-mail: Due to prevalent use of header forgery, mail server investigation and proactive e-mail tracking is frequently used.

> Website users and operators: Should be tactical enough, especially when tracking operators.

> Web based short message service (SMS) sender: Investigators need a full understanding of the service mechanism.

> Mobile device holder: If a mobile device is chosen by a criminal to avoid tracking, locating it usually is extremely vexing work.

The use of automation in digital forensic investigations is not only a technological issue, but also has political and social implications. Current attitudes towards the use of automation in digital forensic investigations are examined, as well as the issue of digital investigators' knowledge acquisition and retention. Highly automated digital forensics – sometimes referred to as "push-button forensics" (PBF) – receives much criticism from the digital investigation community. Criticisms generally appear to focus on two aspects of digital investigations due to inadequate expertise and reliance of PBF and low investigation capacity.

Another challenge is the definition of an experienced investigator. Experience is not the same as competence. Irons, Stephens, et al. (2009) specifically differentiate between practice and theory as well as skills and knowledge when dealing with the training of competent digital investigators, claiming that each area needs to be developed to ensure competency. However, neither Irons nor the UK Forensic Science Regulator focus on the investigator's retention of learned theory and knowledge; only present performance and undefined technical skill maintenance. Similarly, most studies assume that all investigators or technicians are also interested in their job, and are free of possibly undiagnosed psychiatric and learning disorders that can inhibit or prevent learning and retention beyond the basics required for the job1 (Goldstein 1997; Wender, Wolf et al. 2001In these situations, potential evidence may be missed due to disinterest or lack of retention of knowledge.

Just like any profession, expansive expert knowledge cannot come only from the field; it must also come from continued formal and informal study. According Gogolin (2010), "digital skills are perishable if not kept current", and 75% of investigators receive between zero (30% of the sample) and 5 days annual training. Casey (2009) affirms that "there are some fundamental principles, concepts, and skills that everyone in this field must abide by and know". Many investigators have little to no digital investigation training before starting, and even after, "[o]nly 34% of [digital forensic] investigators [surveyed in Michigan, USA] received formal training in laboratory forensics, with the majority being trained 2 weeks or less" (Gogolin 2010).

Theoretical Framework of Forensic investigation

The focus has always been legislation and forensic investigations, rather than adequate collaboration and exchange of intelligence with security students, financial institutions, and network providers for cybersecurity. E-commerce continues to expand the trends of cybercrime, with crimes such as hacking, phishing and even impersonation. Year after year cyber-attacks are been registered. As the cyberspace has become a playground for criminal innovation, evolution and collaboration amongst petty groups in the world.

Criminal profiling and forensic demur a security challenge in some countries. As such, when the police take a step, cybercriminals take 10steps ahead, due to the changing character of crimes to preserve their identity, for the credibility of cybercriminal investigations have always been argued, concerning evidence tendered in court, because of the paradigm shift on both sides. From scamming, hacking, vishing and phishing, the trends keep mutating with Interception, interruption, modification and fabrication of data. Some of the major reasons of this deviant attitude is; flow of income as well as capital flight and banks are reluctant to accept cases cyber-attacks so as to better enforce security and authentication system not sustainable for present cyber battle. The cybercrime tree is best explained with "the 5 stages of cybercrime":

The 5 Stages of Cybercrime[6]

Cybercriminal

- Scammer
- Machine man
- Ngues man
- 419ners
- Sakawa

Redundant service

- Digital connection or wires (internet toolkit, mobile hotspot)
- Electrical appliances (generator, power bank)

Victims

- Mugu
- Maga
- Jk
- Clients
- Banks

Pick-up

- Bank manager or cashier
- Friend in a foreign country
- Friend in the country of residence

Cyber criminality

- Identity theft
- Identity fraud
- Card cloned
- Passport fraud

---

6   The 5 stage of cybercrime came in to existence in 2017 after a field survey of how cybercriminals operate, and through exchange with suspected criminals in Cameroon.

The 5 stages of cybercrime examine the three major actors' concerns with the act. The cybercriminal plays a double role; he assumes the role of an employer, business man or manager and vendor. The victim is always considered as client, buyer or employee to the cybercriminal. The pick-up receives the money as accountant, treasurer or partner, deducts his share or percentage, before expediting back to the cybercriminal. It is considered 5 stage of cybercrime because; reliable service or redundant services are the major tools for crime perpetration, as it also helps dissimulate online information, transaction and forensic evidence. As digital evidence is one of the main challenges as concerns cybercriminal investigations and sometimes need to breach privacy rule.

Email accounts are usually fake, impersonation; transactions usually involve a third party or the use of fake ID cards gotten from dishonest staffs or through unscrupulous ways. Also the way some law enforcement officers receive victims, gives them the impression that nothing can be done. The evolution of cyber criminality is due to inadequate cooperation and training of law enforcement officers, financial institutions and network providers.

The strategic figure for cybercriminal investigation is given opposite;

Law enforcement

- Federal Bureau of Investigation (FBI)
- International Criminal Police (INTERPOL)

Preliminary inquiry from the victim

- Identification document (ID card or Passport)
- Phone number, social insurance number and resident number
- Bank where transaction will be effectuated

Collaboration or intelligence gathering

- Share information with network service providers
- provide financial institutions with criminal database (particularly facial recognition, because fake documents are used to withdraw money)
- reliable complaint center

Forensic Investigation

- Name and phone number of suspect
- IP address track
- E-mail exchange
- Financial transaction records

The Three Stage Model of Cybercriminality[7]

The three stage model explains how the law enforcement must pursuit cybercriminal investigations. The first two stages are the most important, because with data or information forensic is doom to fail. The preliminary stage, help gather information from the victim. Information gotten from the victim should be exploited judiciously by the law enforcement. The second stage is based on intelligence sharing with banks, mobile operators[8] and security students. Intelligence or brief given by a security student on the changing patterns of crime and common groups will aid investigation.

Also, monitoring techniques of banks and mobile operators can gather information about financial transactions, where the transaction was withdrawn, which network was used to perpetrate the crime and how the internet toolkit can facilitate criminal tracking. These boost criminal investigation, for cybercriminals exploit networks (wifi) and cybercafé, which are not usually secured and registered. Privacy is has been evoked as a major challenge to criminal investigation. For instance, the Federal Bureau of Investigation (FBI) had to hire a hacker to breach the security system of an Iphone belonging to a terrorist after the San Bernardino incident.

Security software continues to be purchased each minute from the dark market by cybercriminals at a cheap rate, alongside internet toolkits which facilitates crime commission. Digital evidence remains a myth or doom in relation to investigations by security service concern cyber criminality. Privacy is a major problem raised by some financial institutions and mobile companies for their clients or costumers. As such, cybercriminals are well secured, not only with software acquired in the dark market but also institutions. But to what extend does forensic investigations

---

7   The three stage model of cyber criminality is a procedural method to be used by law enforcement officers to police cybercrime, identity theft, and identity fraud and money laundry.

8   See RSA (2015) CYBERCRIME 2015: An Inside Look at the Changing Threat Landscape

help in cyber criminality? The question is yet to be answered as each day, marks new technological innovations and strategies.

Criminal identification biometrics uses biometric technologies to verify and identify the identity of a suspect, detainee, or individual in order to conduct law enforcement functions. Criminal identification was the first widespread use of biometric technology employed during the decades of the non-automated applications. Over the past 25 years, automated fingerprint searches against state, national and international databases, as well as automated processing of mug shots, have become universal in criminal identification.

The use of biometrics in law enforcement and forensics is quite well known, especially for the identification of criminals. AFIS, the Automated Fingerprint Identification System, in particular has been used to identify criminals for many years by international policing agencies. The fingerprint is a universally recognized method of identification. The American Federal Bureau of Investigation (FBI) has millions of fingerprints on file for conducting searches.

Beyond AFIS, facial-scan is used in criminal identification, but with a lower degree of accuracy; however, it is making good progress in terms of crowd surveillance using CCTV footage, and scanning facial images on internet sites, such as Facebook, to assist in the detection of individuals of interest.

Cybercriminal pattern through mobile money

Mobile money has become a new threat to national and international terrorism, as well as the re-emergence of non-conventional crimes like cybercrime and identity theft. With the cheap rate at which SIM cards are sold and poor identification mechanism in some countries and also available victims because of poor communication of mobile operating companies account for criminal records.

Criminals usually purchase a phone (usually called choroko[9]) from the black market to perpetrate crimes and later resale in the dark market. When they get this phone, the buy sim cards from commercial agents and identify the SIM with the agents identity card, claiming to have forgotten theirs (identity theft), which the use to perpetrate crimes. Others use attestation of lost to identity such SIM cards and create mobile money accounts use for mobile money hits.

Moreover, they sent messages (SMS) to any cell number requesting the person to update or change his mobile money personal identifying number[10] (PIN) following a security modification at the operation center. A code is usually given for the pin to be sent, which after the account is empty by the criminal monitoring the victim from his laptop or phone. They also request the victim (Jk, Maga and Mugu) to effectuate a mobile money transaction to their number following a game the won, as the number of the later was shortlisted by the mobile agency. If the later does this operation using a commercial agent (working for mobile operating company) along the street, the account is immediately emptied.

Law enforcement officers are always left without evidence during criminal investigation because of negligence and inadequate security measures as concerns cyber security. Poor authentication methods[11] and inadequate education for those involved in the battle against non-conventional crimes. As such, police officers turn to track the wrong person, while the criminal continue perpetrating crimes with different identities, can be that of a commissioner or an individual not aware of his name, phone number (cloned[12]) and residence gotten from social media and used by a cybercriminal.

---

9   Choroko is an appellation for phones which are or cannot connect to the internet.

10 Mobile money (MoMo) PIN is a five digit secret code given to each subscriber in order to effectuate financial transactions, purchase airtime and pay bills.

11 As law enforcement officers continue to track cybercriminals, the adopt new strategies; use of fake id cards or attestation of lost for cash withdrawal.

12 Clone a phone number is a criminal pattern of duplicating a sim card.

Cybercriminal

- purchase of sim card registered with someone else name
- purchase of a mobile phone from the black market

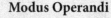

Modus Operandi

- sms requesting the subscriber to update or change mobile money pin or secret code
- sms requesting the subscriber to pay a certain fee to withdraw the cash price because his/her number was shortlisted to win an amount
- A code is sent to play a game or update mobile money account, immediately the code is launched, the clients account is emptied.
- Bank where transaction will be effectuated

Victim

- send his/her pin or validate the code sent by suspected criminal, mobile money account goes red
- when the client or victim send the sum requested by the criminal 'agent of mobile operating company', the number is no more connected to the network.

Criminal Investigation Failure

- withdrawal with mobile money (cash out) does not require ID card
- the sim card and phone are usually disposed after crimes
- the security will be tracking the wrong person, since the sim card was registered by business vendor and the phone will be bought in the dark market by another person.

Identity theft as a challenge to criminal investigators

Identity Thieves

- post kill advertisement of scholar-ships and jobs in foreign countries with accommo-dation with good salary.

Modus Operandi

- request for scan documents such as passport, certificates and accompany by bank transaction or credit card payment.

- request originals to be sent to them for fast visa processing.

- use fake id card or attestation of lost of id card to collect the document in a near by country

- demand huge sum of money in order to return the documents or passport of victim

- they may the passport or other documents to perpetrate crimes abroad.

Challenges

- online calls or virtual numbers used by criminals are usually secured with VPN.

- The issue of privacy demurs a strategic threat to financial and mobile operating companies.

- virtual accounts and staff dishonesty.

Security Pattern

- use of virtual numbers

- after a hit, laptop, phone sim card and other tools are sold to the black market or destroy.

- staff dishonesty is an inevitable issue as concerns transfer of funds by criminals which cannot usually be tracked.

Identity theft has gain ground in developing countries to the extent that people are scared to even register before entering a public organization to visit someone. During a field survey in 2017, found that most victims of identity were targeted through fake scholarship post and U.S DV lottery on social media sites. At this juncture two cases will be explored; scholarship and non-governmental organizations (NGO's).

Scholarship Scam

Cybercriminals post scholarships in to high institutions in foreign countries or defaced website and grab student information through the database of the institution. Most individuals seeking scholarships abroad usually are prey to such patterns. After registration the criminal request for certificates, passport and initial deposited fee nonrefundable for the documents to be studied. They later sends a letter showing the individual has been accepted by the institution and requires he or she to send first installment of fee and original documents so they can easily process the visa from the country where they are, so at the embassy they wouldn't face challenges.

Once they get the original documents and first installment, they frame up issues that there is a mistake in one of the documents and warrants funds to correct. If the client (victim) begins to complaint, blackmail is engaged, all his/ her documents are in the hands and they are operating with different identity and even using the victim's documents to perpetrate crimes. This becomes a phenomenal challenge for law enforcement officers, which at one time tracking criminals and at the same time need to avoid the victim from becoming wanted or recorded as international fugitive, since the documents are used to perpetrate crimes in another continent.

More so, criminals grab such documents and go in for scholarship abroad using another individual's document. Law enforcement officers, embassies and institutions welcoming foreign students should contact the institution and take picture of the new student send to formal institution to find out if is the person or if he/she is found in their database, following the increasing dimension of identity theft in developing countries.

Non-governmental organizations; a new paradigm for cybercriminals

The proliferation of non-governmental organization in developing countries has increase the living standard in some communities, but has also open new criminal tendencies. Criminals launch NGO's to solicit funds from top organization using images of natives in certain of diverse regions in country of residence. They usually grab image from international organization to solicit funds, to be paid in accounts abroad, well as the also use spiritual leaders image to solicit funds or donate. Most of their post on social media sites usually call of subscribers to type 'AMEN' or donate using account similar to that of prominent churches.

Financial crime and identity theft

Cash Withdrawal requirement	Criminal Pattern	Victim
• validate national identity card (ID card) or passport or educational card • sender's identity (name, cell number, state or region) • beneficiary's number and residence (also signatures)	• Use of attestation or lost ID card or scanned copy with name of person • track transactions online and redirect the funds • collaborate with dishonest staff to withdraw the money with certain percentage gain	• identity theft • cybercrime • menace or threat • victim becomes a suspect to law enforcement

Despite the creation of international, regional and national commissions for financial crimes, the challenge keep persisting.

Financial organizations suffer a huge loss every month, money transfer is been tracked as a withdrawn by cybercriminal in partnership with dishonest staffs.

Drawing from an interview with a victim of identity theft and financial fraud, she explains her ordeal; when she got to the bank to withdraw her money, the transaction done from the U.S, she was told the fund had already been withdrawn, her name was shown on the computer, her phone number, but what was not correct on that information was the date and place of birth, parents name and id card number. Probably the criminal grab information produces attestation of lost or scans ID card to withdraw the money. The question of staff dishonest is usually raised as to how can a man withdraw a financial transaction to be done by a woman? How do they procure these documents? Why can't the police track these criminals? These are formidable questions to orientate criminal and forensics investigation. This is because the victim becomes the suspect, and the investigation oriented to the wrong direction.

Financial crimes or fraud go beyond client cash withdrawal, but also attack on international entities and even states. Where a person creates a virtual account in complicity with a bank manager or cashier to gain a contract or to gain a visa to travel abroad, which after a week or a month, some a year and the account is no more credible, there criminal patterns follow. as such, law enforcement officers are always left in the dark. Inadequate training and lack of technological equipment demurs a breach between criminals and the judiciary.

Conclusion

According to Bruce Schneier, 'Security is not a product, it's a process'. For security is not a technological problem, but people and management problem[13]. Modern technology offers myriad options for communication between individuals and among small groups, including cell phones, e-mail, chat rooms, text messaging and various forms of mass media. With voice-over IP (VOIP) telephone service, digital phone calls are becoming indistinguishable from

---

13   See Herhat, J. (2011). Cyber Crime a Growing Challenge for Government.

digital documents both can be stored and accessed remotely. But sensor technology enables the tagging and tracking of information about individuals without their permission or awareness.

Cybercriminal operate like terrorists, in an embedded manner. The idea is that most criminals leave tracks or signature in browsers and networks and might make use of the communications channels available to all. Which is challenging for criminal investigators to extract criminal tracks from non-threat tracks? For example the pressure exerted by the Federal Bureau of Investigation (FBI) on Apple to unlock one of the San Bernardino gunmen iPhone (Tribune News Service, 04.06.16). The FBI equally fired a lawsuit against Apple for the company to create software to unlock iPhone, what a challenge to the organization.

In addition, the cold war among China and U.S, Russia and U.S, North Korea and U.S, has exposed the necessity of cyber warriors for developing countries for future threats. As cybercrime is not limited to individuals but extend to attack on states; the Nigeria secret service database attack. The challenging nature or complexity of cybercrimes warrants security expert and analyst[14]. Experts will expose the tools, tactics and procedure used by criminals to protect their identity. The bank of the suspect, if a credit card or bank transfer was effectuated by suspect, deduct the medium calls where placed (cell phone or digital calls), source of email and text messaging and the internet service providers record online activities.

---

14 In the developed countries they have cyber warriors, trained to secure the country's cyberspace and the ministry of defense against cyber-attacks on strategic data which might pose a threat to national security.

CHAPTER FOUR

PROSTITUTION AND CYBER INSECURITY IN CAMEROON

Prostitution is the act of commercializing oneself for either money or service. Thought legislation's in Cameroon prescribe punishment for prostitution with an amount to be paid and jail sentence, the business still flourishes. Prostitution is one of the largest businesses in the world, which hires millions of women each hour. In Cameroon, the business has gained ground and some suggest space be given to them during the Labour Day parade, since they have the sex hawkers syndicate. The emergence of new forms of crimes like cybercrime and identity theft has been linked to prostitution in Cameroon. Security in Cameroon is faced with two pertinent questions in regards to cyber insecurity; who is a prostitute? What is the role played by prostitutes in cybercrime? The scope of prostitution has increased in Cameroon which is not only limited to street hawkers but also students, workers in mobile operating companies and airtime vendors.

Cyber Insecurity Scenery

The term cyber refers to electronic communication network and virtual reality. The problem under discussion is cyber insecurity which constitute; scamming, phishing, skimming[1] and hacking. According to Law No 2010/012 of 21 December 2010 relating to

---

1 The Director-General of the National Agency for Information and Communication Technologies, Ebot pointed out that, regional banks lost at least CFA 3 billion (more than US$5 million) through deeds of skimming in 2015

cyber security and cyber criminality in Cameroon, cybercrime is defined as an illegal activity related to the internet world or cyberspace committed by an individual or group of persons for financial motives. The have been recent acronyms adopted by criminals like Ngues, machine man, dak just to name a few. Identity theft is a strategy used by individuals to steal data that defines a person. In Cameroon, such activities are oriented on skimming and the use of the SIM box[2] (CAJNews Africa, 2016). According to Arora et al (2012), there exists a vicious circle on the latter. The role of prostitutes in cybercrime in Cameroon is mapped as follows; hacking of accounts and skimming, identity theft on mobile money and offensive content, harassment and drugs.

The Role of Prostitutes in Cyber criminality in Cameroon

The evolution of capitalism has led to increasing level of crimes. Sociologist like Ronald Weitzer pointed out six types of prostitutes in his work titled "Legalizing Prostitution in 2011" which are independent escort, brothel employee, window worker, escort agency employee, casino worker and streetwalker. At this juncture, the role of prostitutes will be examined.

1. Hacking of accounts and skimming

2. Identity theft on mobile money

3. Offensive content, harassment and drugs

1. Hacking of accounts and skimming

With the evolution of information and communication technology the pattern of crimes have changed, with prostitutes engaged in organized crimes such as cybercrime and identity theft. The collaboration of prostitutes and cybercriminals is far beyond the definition of cyber criminality. These prostitutes gather credit card information of their clients such as name and credit card number,

---

2   Sim box or interconnect bypass fraud or SIM bank is a device used as part of VoIP gateway installation which contains a number of Sim cards and use to traffic mobile networks

for accounts to be hacked, some click with dishonest authorities for security.

Moreover, prostitutes engaged in organized crimes get visit cards of their victims which usually contain email, phone numbers, job description, position and order of name for phishing. As such, they contact victims through such mediums, telling him or her the account need to be update, requiring a new password through a form sent through mail. Criminals equally clone credit card and effectuate online wiring. Another pattern is that malicious software are sent to the victim's mail, when he/she clicks the account is pirated. One of the major reasons for the increasing victimization[3] of Cameroonians and foreigner is due to lack of proper security measures by financial institutions, mobile operation companies and state security agencies which rarely caution the population on the evolution of crimes and also their inadequate training accounts for the high vulnerability rate.

Exploring the Stanley Mark Rifkin Case

In 1978, Rifkin moseyed over to Security Pacific's authorized personnel wire-transfer room, where the staff sent and received transfers totaling several billion dollars every day. He was contracted to backup system for the wire transfer room in case breach or attack of their main computer. That role gave him access to the transfer procedures, including how bank officials arrang for transfer to be sent. He learned that bank officers were authorized to order wire transfers would be given a closely guarded daily code each morning to use when calling the wire room.

In the wire room the clerks saved themselves the trouble of trying to memorize each day's code: They wrote down the code on a slip of paper and posted it where they could see it easily. This particular November day Rifkin had a specific reason for his visit. He wanted to get a glance at that paper. Arriving in the wire room, he took some notes on operating procedures, supposedly to make sure

---

3   Broadhurst and Chang (2012) proposed the criminalization of gadgets used by cybercriminals, which will help law enforcement officers in their crack down. For example, toolkit can be equipped with spyware which transfer data to cyber defense center.

the backup system would mesh properly with the regular systems. Meanwhile, he surreptitiously read the security code from the posted slip of paper, and memorized it. As he said afterward, he felt as if he had just won the lottery. There's This Swiss Bank Account...Leaving the room at about 3 o'clock in the afternoon, he headed straight for the pay phone in the building's marble lobby, where he deposited a coin and dialed into the wire-transfer room. He then changed hats, transforming himself from Stanley Rifkin, bank consultant, into Mike Hansen, a member of the bank's International Department.

He changed hats once again to call another department at the bank, this time claiming to be an employee in the wire-transfer room. He obtained the settlement number and called the girl back. She took the number and said, "Thanks." (Under the circumstances, her thanking him has to be considered highly ironic.) A few days later Rifkin flew to Switzerland, picked up his cash, and handed over $8 million to a Russian agency for a pile of diamonds. He flew back, passing through U.S. Customs with the stones hidden in a money belt. He had pulled off the biggest bank heist in history--and done it without using a gun, even without a computer. Oddly, his caper eventually made it into the pages of the Guinness Book of World Records in the category of "biggest computer fraud." Stanley Rifkin had used the art of deception--the skills and techniques that are today called social engineering. Thorough planning and a good gift of gab is all it really took.

2. Mobile Money Accounts (MMA)

There is an adage that "no risk no reward" with the proliferation of mobile operating companies in Cameroon which has made them to engage in banking sector[4]. One of the fastest technique to make profit, with little or no security, enhanced by the android generation in Cameroon. Due to its services like fast money transfer, airtime borrowing and payment of bills. Though this is social development, some Pan Africanists perceive mobile money as a strategy of financing terrorism or terrorist organizations.

---

4   The creation of mobile money accounts is major shift for Cameroon in to the age of technological development.

For instance, senders are not sometimes identified. As such, after discussing with a terrorist organization, the can effectuate a mobile money transaction, since the senders name is not required in some of its transactions.

Furthermore, the quest for profit by mobile operation companies has reduced the level of security protocols for their clients. For example, during an interview with an agent of a mobile operation company in Cameroon involved in mobile money, she said there is no criteria for selection for agents engaged in the task of identifying SIM cards sold at 100 and the registration of airtime vendors which is critical not only to citizens but also to national security. Since most of the works or agents engaged in the task have targets to attain per day, some connive with cybercriminals an identify SIM cards with other people's information. She went ahead to say, some of the agents cooperate with cybercriminals and give valuable information gotten from workers in the company through seduction and they also have a commission.

The pattern changes each hour, as some mobile money agents have become part of the game. In some areas in Cameroon, cybercriminals lull some mobile money agents to get information about their victims. Others buy numbers of people from airtime vendors and use to browse due to the poor networking system and cyber security in the country. In an interview with an agent of a mobile operation company offering this service, the lady said the salary for the job is little as compare to the task involved. As such, in the bid to keep to standard with the capitalists system, ladies go extra mile in to prostitution with business clients of the mobile operating companies to get information and sell to criminals.

An examination of financial crimes in Zimbabwe

Financial exclusion is a major security challenge to development and poverty reduction in developing Countries (Munongo & Bizah, 2017). EcoCash is a mobile payments platform use in Zimbabwe. The globalization era introduced mobile money; a convenient and real-time financial services platform through a mobile telephone. The terms mobile money refers to a set of applications that enable people to use their cell phones to effectuate financial transactions, save money, access credit or insurance products (Donner and Tellez, 2008).

Though mobile money have some interesting features, the Postal and Telecommunications Regulatory Authority of Zimbabwe (POTRAZ, 2014) reported the high rate of mobile telephone penetration (87.3%)Transaction over mobile payments platforms following inception totaled USD $445.7 million in December 2014 (POTRAZ, 2014). This is evidence of the immense potential of mobile banking to harness criminal tendencies. Just like mobile money, EcoCash system has a time- out feature; one need to be really fast when using the application. After seconds an error feedback message is sent to the user, necessitating the user to restart the transaction (Munongo & Bizah, 2017).

An examination of financial crimes in Nigeria

In Nigeria today, numerous internet assisted crimes are committed daily in various forms such as identity theft, cyber harassment, fraudulent electronic mails, Automated Teller Machine spoofing, hacking, phishing and spamming (Okeshola & Adeta, 2013). Usually these crimes are committed in forms like sending of fraudulent and bogus financial proposals from cyber criminals to innocent internet users. In most Nigeria tertiary institutions, various form of crimes are being witnessed ranging robbery and stealing, sexual abuse, assault, cultism amongst others. Cybercrime emerge in the tertiary institutions due to denting and drilling holes in the nation's economy. The emergence of this new 'game' has contributed to the breach of trust with Nigerian commercial companies with many western countries[5].

Perpetrators (yahoo yahoo boys or 419ners) are taking advantage of e-commerce system available on the internet to defraud victims (maga, JK and mugu) thousands and sometimes millions of dollars. They fraudulently represent themselves as having particular goods to sell or that they are involved in a loan scheme project. They may

---

5   France today requires web camera verification for most online business transactions from Nigeria (Okeshola &Adeta, 2013).

pose to have financial institution where money can be loaned out to prospective investors. In this regard, so many persons have been duped. But this could not only be the techniques used by these cyber criminals.

According to a publication by Economic and Other Financial Crime Commission in Nigeria named Zero Tolerance (2006), stated that a retired civil servant with two (2) other accomplices defrauded a German citizen name Klaus Wagner a sum of USD 1, 714,080 through the internet. Internet Crime Report of 2007, shortlisted Nigeria amongst the leading countries in terms of cybercrime (Sesan, 2010). Ribadu (2007) stated that the prominent forms of cybercrime in Nigeria are cloning of websites, false representations, internet purchase and other e – commerce kinds of fraud. Olugbodi (2010), states that the most prevalent forms of cybercrime are website cloning, financial fraud, identity theft, credit card theft, cyber theft, cyber harassment, fraudulent electronic mails, cyber laundering and virus/ worms/ Trojans.

3. Drug, offensive content and harassment

Drug, harassment and offensive content are gaining grounds in Cameroon. It has been linked to cybercrime, as criminals keep bullying lecturers, foreigners and stakeholders in the country. In Cameroon foreigners (Bushfallers) are most targeted persons when discussing of drug, offensive content and harassment. Two cases will be explored at this level, first that of a university lecturer of the state and a foreigner which are unreported.

Case study 1: Offensive content and harassment of university lecturer

Sexual harassment is one of the leading issue in secondary and university milieu. In 2014, a young lady obtain her first degree in a state university, when the lecturer who was harassing her had his naked pictures with some suspected criminals working with the girl blackmailing the latter to pay a certain amount and she must have the first degree if not he will be exposed and pictures published in all social platforms. The lecturer was faced with a huge challenge, first that of offensive content and harassment then extortion. Though the act committed by the lecturer is punishable, it's still rampant in the academic milieu and as well the young lady can be imprisoned for extortion as per section 318 of the Cameroon Penal code. But she obtained the first degree and left to do her master's in a private university in the country.

Case study 2: Drug and harassment of foreigners (Bushfaller)

The industrial revolution revolutionized the world, as thing that were done by hand were now produce or made by machine. Some Africans consider the West as utopia. As such, any person from the West is like a semi god in Cameroon. But criminals collaborate with young ladies from universities and secondary schools to drug this foreigners (Bushfallers) to take their passport and other documents and start harassing them to pay huge sums of money in order to recover their documents or they will burn it into ashes.

This case is rampant with guys from the US and other European countries. During this period, they use phone booth (call box) for security purposes.

Also, they collaborate with some dishonest staffs[6] (back up or pick-up) of financial institutions to receive the money. It will be recalled that, though the is legislation which deals with illicit drug trafficking, offensive content and harassment, these crimes keep increasing at a geometric rate in Cameroon because of negligence and lack of cooperation.

Conclusion

The complexity of cybercrime, requires adequate knowledge and expertise to crackdown criminals. It should be noted that one of the major issue with cyber insecurity in Cameroon is prostitution. The lack of collaboration among stakeholders, mobile operating

---

6   See CIFAS and CIPD (2012) Staff fraud and dishonesty managing and mitigating the risk, Guide June 2012

companies, financial institutions and security experts accounts for cyber insecurity in the country. As such, the Cameroon government should introduce cyber security as a course in the police academy, so as to educate them on the changing patterns and gadgets used by cybercriminals and identity thieves in Cameroon. Also, mobile operating companies should boost the client security relationship rather than focusing on profit. For there is a say that the client is the king and should be treated as such.

Olowu (2009)on his part, observed that the unemployment rate in several African countries most of whom are graduates and literate in computing and internet skills is an influential factor for the existence and growth of cybercrimes. The poor politics of development, poverty and lose of welfare has led youths into street culture in urban towns and particularly for graduates, cybercrimes is an alternative to have access to quick finance. The use of spyware will help track down hackers and dishonest staff who try to modify, fabricate or delete data from the database of transactions that can be used as evidence in a law suit. This issue facilitates research because the law enforcement agencies continue to face security challenges such as the identification and geographical locations and strategies of cybercriminals. Affected botnet provides them with exact information and evidence.

CHAPTER FIVE

CYBER TERRORISM, CYBERATTACK AND RADICALISM

The Internet has innumerable positive features, but it also provides a platform for criminal activities like terrorism, cyber-attacks and radicalization. In the 1990s, the main concern was that terrorist organizations might launch network-based attacks against critical infrastructure, such as transportation and energy supply ("cyber terrorism"). This view of terrorist use of the Internet began to change after the 2001 attacks in the United States. Although the 9/11 attacks were not cyber-attacks, the perpetrators used the Internet extensively in planning and financing the operation and in communicating with their hierarchy.

In 2005, the United Nations Counter-Terrorism Implementation Task Force (CTITF) was established to ensure overall coordination and coherence in the counter-terrorism efforts of the United Nations system in collaboration with the International Criminal Police (INTERPOL). The United Nations Global Counter-Terrorism Strategy, which brings together into one coherent framework decades of United Nations counter-terrorism policy and legal responses emanating from the General Assembly, the Security Council and relevant United Nations specialized agencies, has been the focus of the work of CTITF since its adoption by the General Assembly in September 2006 (General Assembly resolution 60/288).

The Strategy sets out a plan of action for the international community based on four pillars[1]:

- Measures to address the conditions conducive to the spread of terrorism;

- Measures to prevent and combat terrorism;

- Measures to build States' capacity to prevent and combat terrorism and to strengthen the role of the United Nations system in this regard;

- Measures to ensure respect for human rights for all and the rule of law as the fundamental basis of the fight against terrorism.

The institutionalization of CTITF within the United Nations Secretariat, the Secretary-General in 2009 established a CTITF Office within the Department of Political Affairs to provide support for the work of CTITF on a number of thematic initiatives under the policy guidance of Member States through the General Assembly. CTITF also seek to foster constructive engagement between the United Nations system, international and regional organizations, the private sector, and civil society on the implementation of the Strategy.

The March 2009 Report of the CTITF Working Group revealed that, training, recruitment, datamining, propaganda and radicalization were carried by terrorist organization with the use of internet. Several security measures were tabled on these issues, but it diverse landscape keep mutating. As the Internet is based on technology, the debate has tended to focus on technical countermeasures such as the blocking of websites; but it goes beyond that. The 2009 Report of the CTITF Working Group, expose some legal prescriptions to consider. Thus, a structural definition of "terrorism" and "terrorist intent", issues such as the protection of human rights, the legality

---

1   See; United Nations Counter-Terrorism Implementation Task Force report on Countering the Use of the Internet for Terrorist Purposes —Legal and Technical Aspects, May 2011

of investigative instruments and the applicability of criminal law provisions in counter-terrorist work, are also relevant.

The Working Group recognizes that the use of the Internet for terrorist purposes cannot be addressed nor resolved solely through legal solutions alone: any effective approach must include a solid understanding and appreciation of the technical aspects of ICT (information and communications technology). In order to ensure such a comprehensive approach, the Working Group held a second workshop of international experts in Redmond, Washington (USA) in February 2010 which was hosted by the Microsoft Corporation. United Nations Office on Drugs and Crime (UNODC).

Cyberterrorism Theory

Cyberterrorism theory focuses on doctrine, command and time. It explores the socio-political and economic motivation of attacks on computers, networks and information which causes physical injury by radicals or sovereignty free actors. The interest in cyberterrorism is the quest to showcase Muslim supremacy (radical Muslim) and unity through the 'Jihad'. Unity is express through the doctrine of jihad (considered as a holy war by radical Muslims) and rhetorical condemnation of Western education. These threats are mostly coordinated by radical Muslim cleric or imams (Imam Abubakar Shekau of Boko-Haram, American-born radical imam Anwar al-Awlaki played a critical role in recruiting and equipping Umar Farouk Abdulmutallab in 2009 failed attack in U.S and Imam Samudra of 2002 Bali bombing) who advocate for physical violence and terror in the world.

Command and time remain two strategic factors of cyberterrorism. It's not only limited to science, resources, courage and speed (timing) to carry out acts of terror. As most individuals involved in cyberterrorism, have gone through formal education in IT (computer science, computer engineering, and information science) and security studies (information security and network security) (Dorothy E. Denning, The Jihadi Cyberterror Threat). Knowledge and expertise of this sovereignty free actors (radicals,

91

terrorists or militia) security threats increase at a geometrical rate after the 9/11 attacks in U.S. As new groups (Islamic State, Boko-Haram, Al Shabaab and Al Qaeda in the Islamic Magreb) have emerged with different patterns of attacks either physical or through the cyberspace, as time remains a formidable factor in attacks. Resources are generated through sympathizers and from cyber-attacks (coordinated by hackers of terrorist organizations) on financial and security institutions. Media couvrage (blogs, website and even chatrooms) has increased alongside the recruitment

Doctrine

- Teachings of radical Islam by some imams

- The culture of some muslims jihad, proclamation of a caliphate

- Secessionist ideas initiated by individuals in foreign nations, to destabilize their country.

Command

- Love and respect for the leader

- Knowledge or expertise in science by terrorist or agents of terrorist organizations (hired hackers)

- Resources (financial resource and material resource)

Time or Timing

- When attacks are been coordinated for example 9/11 in U.S., Charlie Hebdo in France and the 2017 attack near the World Trade Center appeal for proper security measures.

- Jihadi John beheading some individuals expresses acts of terror on the cyberspace of individuals, as well as training being posted online on how to produce weapons and where it should be dropped.

The 9/11 attacks in U.S. change the dynamics of international security and terrorism due to its media coverage. Aircrafts flew into the Twin Tower and the World Trade Center under the commander of Osama Bin Laden, which left serious civilian casualties and damage. As such, terrorist organization continues to aspire to stage attacks against the Western world. Training and sponsorship of these organizations remains rhetoric to the international community, as recruitment double each year on social media. For example, Colleen LaRose (Jihad Jane) engaged in Islamic radicalism over the internet due to her marriage separation (Reyes, 2016). She welcomed ideology of some radicals due to her emotional state and access to available online community of radical Islamists. As a teen (16 years) in a union with a 32-year-old man, she was exposed to petty crimes such as writing bad checks, which is a strategic element for terrorist networks.

The relevance of this theory as concerns terrorism is to caution statesmen and security experts about the security threats posed by migration and multiculturalism. That is, communication (the case of secessionist) and integration or recognition of person's in a society is of vital importance in combating cyberterrorism and other non-conventional crimes. The theory also advocates for proper surveillance and background check of foreign students engage in the field of IT and Security Studies in affected countries to restrain future security threats. For example, Mohammed Emwazi (Jihadi John) IT graduate in England, who claimed the security services were ruining his life and Sami Omar Al-Hussayen Saudi CS graduate student at university of Idaho studying computer security, charged for operating websites used to recruit terrorists, raise funds, and disseminate inflammatory rhetoric[2].

The Globalization Era

Rapid developments in technology is a challenge as well as a tool for global efforts to counter terrorism. While the vast number of

---

2   Read Dorothy E. Denning, The Jihadi Cyberterror Threat

peaceful social causes and political crusaders have benefited from new technologies, evidence shows that terrorist groups do exploit social media communities, for recruitment, fund raising, and propaganda.

As sovereignty free actors take advantage of technical tools to organize, plan and raise funds to support their activities, their increasing reliance also makes them vulnerable to government scrutiny. Governments are increasingly developing sophisticated techniques to identify and track potential terrorists. Rapid advances in technology also permit non-governmental organizations and researchers to detect and monitor the online activities of suspected terrorists in cyberspace. Thousands of suspected terrorist websites have been catalogued by various entities around the world.

Technology alone is no panacea for combating terrorism, including terrorist use of the Internet. Technical approaches should be enshrined in appropriate legal frameworks, which in turn should be part of a comprehensive public policy response that support and clarify the role of technology in combating and countering terrorist activity on the Internet. There is a need for enhanced cooperation between the public and private sectors; as most of the technical infrastructure upon which terrorists are planning, financing and supporting their illegal activities is owned wholly or in part by private entities, there is a strong need to leverage existing expertise within the private sector and for increased information-sharing among stakeholders. If close cooperation between the public and private sectors is adequate progress could be made against terrorist use of the Internet. There is an important role for technology not just in the identification of and response to terrorist use of the Internet, but also in countering the narratives of terrorist groups.

Challenges involved in combating cybercrime and terrorist activities

Strategies to fight cybercrime in general and terrorist use of the Internet in particular currently attract a lot of attention. The reason for this is not just that some of the methods are new and therefore require intensive research, but also that the investigation of crimes involving network technology—such as use of the Internet for terrorist purposes—presents particular difficulties. Some of these arise from the ability of offenders to use software tools—such as those designed to locate open ports or break password protection—while committing an offence.

In addition, an offender who plans an attack can find detailed information on the Internet that explains how to build a bomb. Although information like this was available before the Internet was developed, it was much more difficult to access. Discussion on the correct legal response ranges from a criminalization of the production, sale or even possession of tools primarily designed to commit sophisticated computer attacks, to criminalizing the publication of critical information.

Another challenge is related to the identification of suspects. Although users leave multiple traces while using Internet services, offenders can hinder investigations in particular by disguising their identity. Some countries address these challenges by implementing legal restrictions[3].

Offenders also use automation to scale up their activities, such as hacking attacks. Up to 80 million hacking attacks occur every day, due to the availability of software tools that can attack thousands of computer systems in hours. It is not only automation that causes difficulties in investigating and preventing such attacks. Analysis of the attacks suggests that they were committed by thousands of computers within a "botnet", or group of compromised computers running programs under external control[4].

---

3   China has its own social networking sites to reduce the high risk of online crimes. Italy has also increased her policing methods as public Internet access providers are required to identify users before allowing them access different sites.

4   Offenders use "botnets" to perpetrate powerful attack against computer systems like in Estonia in April 2007.

Terrorist Financing

The 9/11 attacks introduced a taskforce to track terrorists funding and financial transactions (Jialun Qin et al., 2006) (Brian Krebs, 2007). The uncertainty vis-à-vis the scope and extent of the use of the Internet for terrorist financing purposes, many experts believe that funds transfers for terrorist purposes are predominately in cash.

However, as terrorist organizations and their financiers seek ways to disguise and conceal the source of terrorist financing, Internet payment systems will likely play a greater role as they offer a number of advantages to terrorist financiers[5].The United Arabic Emirates Federal Law No 2 of 2006 on Prevention of Information Technology Crime. Instruments to enable competent authorities to confiscate property of value are contained, also the Council of Europe Convention on Laundering, Search, Seizure and Confiscation of the Proceeds from Crime and the Financing of Terrorism.

The use of the internet for Terrorist activities

Evidence that a number of terrorist organizations fund their activities by engaging in traditional forms of online criminality, such as credit card fraud and intellectual property theft. In June 2007, three British residents, Tariq al-Daour, Waseem Mughal, and Younes Tsouli, were charged with using the Internet to incite murder.

Evidence exposed the use of stolen credit card information to purchase goods such as night vision goggles, global positioning devices, airplane tickets and prepaid mobile phone cards to provide direct tactical support for terrorist operations. The trio reportedly made fraudulent charges totaling more than 3 .5 million U.S. dollars and was in possession of a database containing nearly 40,000 stolen credit card accounts (Brian Krebs, 2007).

---

5   Terrorist organizations make use of electronic payment systems to enable online donations. They create websites and publish information on how to make donations and how to join the organization.

In another case, Bali Bomber Imam Samudra funded his attack in which more than 200 people were murdered with an estimated $150,000 US, which he obtained by hacking into Western bank accounts and credit lines[6]. Moreover, Samudra wrote a book while in jail in which he shared his hacking and "carding" techniques with his disciples, encouraging them to take their "holy war" to cyberspace by committing credit card fraud[7]. Participants noted the existence of the vast, organized, cybercrime underground— one which was willing to sell its services to the highest bidder, regardless of ideology or agenda.

Thus, the unanimous concern regarding terrorist organizations leveraging the technical talents of existing organized cyber criminals. Cybercriminal groups, particularly those in Eastern Europe and parts of Asia, widely advertised sophisticated cyberattacks tools, such as "botnets" for rent or sale on the Internet. The increasing concern is due to no available evidence presented to prove terrorists links to hackers of organized crime groups to conduct an advanced technical attack against a target of interest. Offensive cybercrime tools developed by organized crime makes a powerful addition to the arsenal of terrorist tools and time a formidable factor for terrorists to adapt to these capabilities.

The Internet as an Open Source Information Tool for Terrorist Attacks

The globally distributed network has created new opportunities for terrorists to research potential target[8]. According to media

---

6   Read Dorothy E. Denning; The Jihadi Cyberterror Threat http://www.nps. navy.mil/da/faculty/DorothyDenning/index.htm dedennin@nps.edu

Also see; http://news.discovery.com/tech/internet-fraud-finances-terrorism. html.

7   Book chapter in Me Against the Terrorist! He advocates cyber-attacks and evokes fundamentalist's torts against the protein alliance system (that is America and its allies).

8   Through the Internet sovereignty free actors get detailed building schematics, photographs and even satellite couvrage to perpetrate attacks. In 2006 an Al-Qaida affiliate produced a 26-page manual on how to exploit the Google search engine for jihadist tendencies.

reports, during a 2007 operation in Basra, Iraq, British Army officials discovered numerous Google Earth printouts which showed in great detail buildings inside the British base in Basra, with tented accommodations, lavatory blocks and light armored vehicles clearly marked. Based upon further evidence uncovered, British officials deduced the information was being used to plan an attack on their base. In other cases, such as the 2007 planned attempt by terrorists to blow up fuel tanks at New York's John F. Kennedy International Airport, court records indicate that terrorists utilized Google Earth as a means of obtaining detailed aerial photographs of their intended target[9].

Furthermore, evidence from the 2009 attacks in Mumbai, India indicated that terrorists used a wide variety of open source Internet tools, including Google Earth and Maps to plan their assault on the city. Terrorists can also mine a variety of other sources, such as social networking sites, to uncover the names and addresses of individuals affiliated with a target, such as hotel or embassy staff, as well as data on their family connections and their networks.

Data mining is emerging as a major security challenge in the world. The Internet allows both the public and private sector to put vast amounts of information online. While doing so has provided significant cost savings, it has also created significant opportunities for terrorists and others to conduct data mining operations, searching out with precision, the exact details needed to coordinate an attack.

In a January 2003 report, the United States Secretary of Defense warned his personnel that at least 700 gigabytes of Defense Department data was publicly available on government websites and that one needed to assume that this data was being accessed by terrorists to gain insight into the department's plans, programs and activities (McCullagh, Declan, 2003).

Moreover, an Al Qaida training manual uncovered in Afghanistan advised terrorists that by "using public sources openly and without resorting to illegal means, it is possible to gather at least 80 percent

---

9   See; http://news.cnet.com/8301-10784_3-9725253-7.html.

of information about the enemy."[10] In addition, incidents such as the 2011 "Wikileaks" disclosures, which unveiled more than 250,000 diplomatic cables, provide government assessments on the state of terrorist organizations, their plans and intentions, and therefore reveal the extent of their knowledge[11]. This have made some counterterrorism experts to refer to the Internet as a "terrorist university," a place where terrorists learn new techniques and skills to coordinate attacks.

Identity & Attribution

In 1990s, during the age of technological innovation, cartoonist Peter Steiner drew a cartoon for the New Yorker magazine of two dogs sitting in front of a computer screen. One dog, touting the advantages of the new medium, happily told the other "On the Internet, nobody knows you're a dog." The cartoon demonstrates one of the primary advantages and disadvantages of Internet communication: 'anonymity'. The anonymous nature of the Internet has been a boon for people all over the world seeking or posting political, religious, or even medical information and many view anonymity on the Internet as promoting freedom of speech and human rights. Conversely, both criminals and terrorists have used the anonymity for criminal patterns and impunity. Today's online identity challenges stem from the fact that when the original Internet architecture was conceived and constructed, no rigorous means of identification was engineered into the network itself.

However, the Internet does provide for a means of numeric identification via an Internet protocol address, a unique identifier which is transmitted with every step taken on the Internet and which allows the Internet to route traffic to the appropriate destination. Just as each telephone has a unique numeric identifier, so too does each Internet connection. Thus, for example, an

---

10 See "Dot-Com Terrorism," The New Atlantis, Number 5, Spring 2004, pp. 91–93, available at: http://www.thenewatlantis.com/publications/dot-com-terrorism.

11 http://www.guardian.co.uk/world/2010/nov/28/how-us-embassy-cables-leaked.

Internet protocol address is routinely attached to an email to show the source network and user from whom the mail was sent.

From an investigative perspective, it is of course useful to know the Internet protocol address of an email sent, as it can potentially lead to the real-world location of a criminal or terrorist. Unfortunately, knowing that an email may have originated from any particular domain does not tell investigators who may have sent that email, as internet protocols can be changed using diverse software.

Many terrorists are well aware of the Internet protocol addressing system and take steps to ensure their location data is not transmitted as part of their online activities. Simple solutions are to send emails from anonymous cyber-cafes, unsecured wireless access points, or through previously hacked or compromised computers belonging to third parties. Often criminals and terrorists will purposefully route their Internet traffic through multiple countries and jurisdictions, making their communications nearly impossible to trace.

More so, sophisticated methods exist to remain anonymous online, including through the increasing number of cost free anonymization services such as the Hide My Ass, I2P Network and the Tor Project, each of which uses a variety of peer-to-peer and encryption technologies to hide Internet protocol addresses. These anonymization services utilize a proxy server computer that acts as an intermediary and a privacy shield between the client computer and the rest of the Internet. In effect, the proxy acts on the original user's behalf to protect any personal information from being shared with destination points on the Internet beyond the proxy, and as such, users are able to "spoof" or alter their IP address. These proxy services have increased in sophistication in recent years and now often utilize a peer-to-peer networking approach to prevent the user's identity from remaining in any single central third-party site that could disclose a user's identity.

More and more mobile phones are providing access to the Internet and the wide availability of non-registered SIM cards in many countries allows users to make phone calls, send text messages and surf the Internet without any form of identification required.

In addition, the wide availability of "bullet-proof" hosted cloud computing resources means that terrorists are able to host their propaganda and digital content online with little fear of identification or reprisal.

Anonymity in cyberspace makes it vastly more difficult to attribute criminal or terrorist activities to any one group or individual. The lack of attribution techniques was viewed as one of the major obstacles in effectively responding to terrorist use of the Internet.

Without attribution, it was impossible to determine if a particular cyber-attack or intrusion was the work of a lone teenage hacker testing his skills, an international organized crime group seeking to commit a major financial fraud, a terrorist entity launching a denial of service attack against a vital critical infrastructure or a nation state engaging in cyber-warfare. From a technical perspective, the Dark Web Terrorism Research project which allowed investigators to use artificial intelligence and language analysis techniques to improve identification of terrorists in online forums. Terrorists use widely available technical tools, such as data encryption, to obscure and protect their activities. For example, Ramzi Yousef, convicted for his involvement in the first World Trade Center Bombing in 1993, used encryption to hide details of a plot to destroy U.S. Airliners. Police discovered the encrypted files on a computer in his Manila apartment in 1995. Another terrorist, Wadih El Hage, who was indicted for the 1998 bombings of two United States embassies in East Africa sent encrypted e-mails to associates in Al-Qaida according to court papers.

Terrorists can also use other data encryption techniques to keep their communications secret, such as multiple encryptions of the same files. Much like a Matryoshka doll, an encrypted file can be contained within an encrypted file, hidden within another encrypted file, making decryption all but impossible. Former British Airways employee Rajib Karim who allegedly exchanged electronic messages with an Al-Qaida cleric in Yemen in 2010 utilized such a technique. Karim plead guilty in November 2010 to a variety of terrorist charges and was reported to have used multiple encryption techniques to protect 320 gigabytes of data files, including the use of complex ciphers, nested-encryption and data-obfuscation.

Law enforcement officials are attempting to improve their skills in Steganalysis, the craft of uncovering and revealing the use of steganography, but so far there is no consistently available tool for detecting the use of steganography in a computer file Another online technique terrorists can utilize to their advantage is the growing number of places to hide on the Internet. In other words, the sheer volume of data being produced every day is so large, with so many new programs, websites, chat program and microblogging sites emerging, that it has become increasingly easy merely to hide within the noise.

Exploring Umar Farouk A. Case (affiliation Al Qaeda)

Intelligence led security is another word that is popular with security experts or strategists. Security service use intelligence as pro-active measures in disrupting potential eminent threats[12]. It has been used in the UK to justify the arrest of (Muslim) Manchester United fans who were suspected of wanting to blow up Old Trafford the 'Plane Bomb plot' that was said to have been initiated in Pakistan, which led to the ban on carrying liquids into planes. It is intelligence led security that initiated measures such as the national database, the biometric ID cards and the gathering of information through a myriad persons. There has been a simple and yet insight misinterpretation of 'information' and 'intelligence'. It is certainly easy, to gather considerable information on a massive amount of people. However, that cannot be considered to be 'intelligence' until each piece of information is classified, assessed, and put into a wider context. Information gathering is mean less in preventing terrorism unless their modus operandi is exposed, then the data or information becomes valuable. The official Congressional Report on the intelligence failure that led to 9/11 identified the fact that there was so much unassessed data in the system, that there was no way of knowing what was significant[13]. The FBI claimed that there

---

12 Terrorism an Intellectual War by Saron Messembe Obia

13 Ibid 84

are 500,000 people on their 'terrorist watch' list, and therefore they were not able to identify Abdulmutallab as someone of being beyond normal interest, which demonstrates that the attempts to gather more data in order to make itself more effective has actually increased vulnerability[14].

Umar Farouk Abdulmutallab would have been able to carry out his plot without the aid of al-Qaeda in the Arabian Peninsula. More specifically, American-born radical imam Anwar al-Awlaki played a critical role in recruiting and equipping him. Al Awlaki has been given the moniker 'the bin Laden of the internet' according to Al Arabiyah Television. His exploits have been significant enough for President Obama to order the targeted killing of al-Awlaki, the first U.S. citizen to be placed on this list. Abdulmutallab allegedly first met with al-Awlaki in 2005 while Abdulmutallab was in Yemen to study Arabic[15]. In October 2009 Abdulmutallab traveled to a house owned and operated by al Awlaki in the Shabwah Mountains of Yemen. There he received equipment and training in the use of explosives. It is unlikely that Abdulmutallab would have been able to procure PETN, the highly explosive substance used in his attempted attack, without the assistance of an organized terrorist group. Only al-Awlaki, of AQAP could facilitate procurement of the substance. The Muslim community had little impact of Abdulmutallab's progression toward violence. He attended thrilling sermons at various mosques, during his studies of Arabic at a language institute in Sana'a, as the president of the University College of London's Islamic Society. Abdulmutallab boarded Flight 253 without a passport, identifying him as a Sudanese refugee[16]. As the airline often allows Sudanese refugees to fly without passports. Mueller (2011) postulated that, Muslim community involvement identified through radical imams like Anwar al-Awlaki, recruiter for al-Qaeda. Education and refugee status had a great impact in

---

14 Rubens, D. (2009) Umar Farouk Abdulmutallab and the Christmas Day Attack: Why Aren't Lessons Learned?

15 SeeCase 33: The Underwear Bomber by John Mueller, July 12, 2011

16 Abdulmutallab's Sudanese refugee status appeals to intelligence services on policing method in regard to the present refugee crisis in Europe which remains an eminent threat to national security.

Abdulmutallab's penetration in to America, due to intelligence failure.

U.S. Department of Homeland Security report from late 2010 uncovered numerous cases of suspected terrorists sharing operational data in multiple languages on social networking sites, such as methods for building improvised explosive devices (IEDs). Social networking services have all the features of standard websites, and more, allowing terrorists to use them for propaganda, training, recruitment, fund raising, secret communication, data mining and radicalization. Some terrorist groups, however, remain suspicious of social networking sites such as Facebook, and have specifically warned fellow extremists to avoid organizing on the site for fear of detection.

In a prescient October 2008 report, one country's military intelligence officials noted the possibility for terrorists to exploit micro blogging sites such as Twitter, to aid them in conducting real-time terrorist operations. Just one month later a group of terrorists attacked numerous locations in Mumbai, India, and used all the advanced information technologies available to them in an attempt to gain an operational advantage over police, the military and their victims. As well as using Google Earth satellite imagery and handheld GPS devices to plan and perpetrate their attack, 57 reports indicate that they received live updates from their handlers on their Blackberry mobile phones with regard to the location of hostages, especially foreigners. The Mumbai attacks were also noteworthy for the vast use of social media by the public to document the event.

Social networking services provide significant intelligence to terrorists in cyberspace. Users freely share vast amounts of personal information in social networking spaces making it easy to find many targets of interest, such as the names of diplomats working at an embassy, as well as their pictures and those of their spouses and children. In response, numerous governments, especially military officials, have issued warnings to their personnel to be circumspect concerning data they reveal on Facebook, Twitter, and other networks.

Just as social networks provide rich target data to potential terrorists, so too can they yield numerous leads for law enforcement and security officials. Terrorists who participate in social media sites subject themselves to potential social network analysis techniques in which an entire network of friends, family and contacts can be mapped out by officials for identification, 62 providing a powerful tool in the fight against terrorism, especially when used in combination with large data sets of terrorist Internet activity such as Europol's "Check the Web" project or the University of Arizona's "Dark Web" program. Moreover, governments can also leverage social media to their advantage as a means of delivering a counter narrative to the terrorist and extremist ethos, as does one noted program in Indonesia.

Conclusion

Technology proves to be a double-edged sword in the fight against terrorism. Sovereignty free actors have realized its potential and use technological tools for their communications, training, propaganda, recruitment, fundraising and operational planning. Conversely, government security and law enforcement officials can leverage these tools as well to gain greater insight into terrorist activities.

Privacy and human rights is another challenging issues in the fight against modern security threats. As new electronic devices enter the market, human security is instantly threatened by using internet patterns like cyberbullying or cyber-attack. The proliferation of mobile phone, CCTV systems, laptops, personal device assistant (PDA), wireless gaming systems, and electronic financial transactions has increased the level of vulnerability of population as most transnational organizations operate with individuals capable of leveraging such technologies to their advantage.

Public Private Partnership demurs a formidable narrative for counter terrorism. Given that the majority of the infrastructure that underpins global information and communication systems is owned and managed by the private sector, governments should consider partnering in order to formulate strategic responses to the terrorist threat. Governments may explore opportunities to improve information-sharing, both between the public and private sectors and with relevant non-governmental organizations, particularly civil society institutions to discuss on terrorist chat rooms and tracking the online activities of terrorists in cyberspace.

Terrorists have considerably updated their modus operandi to leverage technology to their full advantage of addressing technical issues in countering terrorist use of the Internet, technology alone will not solve this problem. Even when the right technical tools are in place, further human analysis is required to respond to terrorist activity in cyberspace. For these reasons, a multi-pronged approach will undoubtedly be required to deal with terrorist use of the Internet. In order to counter the use of the internet for terrorist purposes more effectively, governments must consider an approach that combines legal, technical and ideological components.

REFERENCES

Abia et al (2010) Cameroonian youths, their attractions to scamming and strategies to divert attention. International NGO Journal. Vol.5 (5), pp.110-116, June 2010.

Adler, P. A., & Adler, P. (2005). Self-injurers as loners: The social organization of solitary deviance. Deviant Behavior, 26(4), 345–378.

Adler, P. A., & Adler, P. (2008). The cyber worlds of self-injurers: Deviant communities, relationships, and selves. Symbolic Interaction, 31(1), 33–56.

Akin, T. (2011). Cybercrime: Response, investigation, and prosecution. Encyclopedia of Information Assurance. New York: Taylor and Francis.

Akuta et al (2011) Combating Cyber Crime in Sub-Sahara Africa; A Discourse on Law, Policy and Practice. Journal of Research in Peace, Gender and Development. Vol.1 (4) pp.129-137, May 2011

Alghafli, K. A., Jones, A., & Martin, T. A. (2011). Guidelines for the digital forensic processing of smartphones. 9th Australian Digital Forensics Conference, SECAU Security Research Centre, Edith Cowan University, Perth, Western Australia.

Allen, G. (2005). Responding to cybercrime: A delicate blend of the orthodox and the alternative. New Zealand Law Review, 2, 149-178.

Allison, R. (2003, October 18). Youth cleared of crashing American port's computer. The Guardian.

Aluko M. (2004) 17 way of stopping financial corruption in Nigeria. www.ComCast.net April 5, 2010

Amichai-Hamburger, Y. (Ed.) (2005). The social net: Understanding human behavior in cyberspace. Oxford University Press.

Amiel, T., & Sargent, S. L. (2004). Individual differences in Internet usage motives. Computers in Human Behavior, 20, 711–726.

Andersen, C. (2014) Games of Drones: The Uneasy Future of the Soldier-Hero in Call of Duty: Black Ops II. Surveillance & Society 12(3): 36-376. http://www.surveillance-and-society. org

Anderson, D. (2015, June 11). A Question of Trust – Report of the Investigatory Powers Review. Independent Reviewer of Terrorism Legislation.

Anderson, K. (2001, August 30). Battling online hate. BBC News Online-World, Americas. Retrieved August 26, 2009 from http://news.bbc.co.uk/2/low/americas/1516271.stm

Andy Sherman, Hillary Clinton Claims Donald Trump Invited Russian President Vladimir Putin to Hack Americans, Politifact (Sept. 26, 2016), http://www.politifact.com/truth-o meter/statements/2016/sep/26/hillaryclinton/hillary-clinton-claims-donald-trump-invited-russia/.

Anonymous (2015, June 20). Quantum computers - A little bit, better. The Economist. Retrieved on 21st June 2015 from http://www.economist.com/news/science-andtechnology/21654566-afterdecades-languishing-laboratory-quantum-computers-areattracting

Apro et al (2005). Hackers: The Hunt for Australia's Most Infamous Computer Cracker. Rowville, Vic: Five Mile Press

Arora, S., Bhatt, Ch. & Pant, A. (2012) Forensics Computing-Technology to Combat Cybercrime. Journal of Advanced Research in Computer Science and Software Engineering. Vol 2, Issue 7, July 2012.

Ash, S. (2002, May 16). Hate groups use Internet to recruit. The Record Kitchener, Ontario, p. B-3.

Ballin, H., & Ballin, M. F. H. (2012). Anticipative criminal investigation - Rule of law principles for counterterrorism. The Hague, Netherlands: T.M.C. Asser Press.

Banks, A. (2014, November 10). Stop and Search Under Fire. The Western Australian. Retrieved on 11th November 2014 fromhttp://au.news.yahoo.com/thewest/a//newshome/7564062/stop-andsearch-laws-under-fire/.

Barlow, J. P. (1992). Decrypting the puzzle palace. Communications of the ACM, 35(7), 2531.

Barrett, J., & Kippler, G. (2010). Virtualization and Forensics: A digital forensic investigator's guide to virtual environments. Boston: Syngress.

Bargh, J. A., & McKenna, K. Y. A. (2004). The internet and social life. Annual Review of Psychology, 55(1), 573–590.

BBC (British Broadcasting Corporation) Africa News (2003). Nigeria to tackle internet frauds. One Minute World News.

BBC News. (2004, April 20). Internet driving hate site surge. BBC News. Retrieved August 26, 2009 from http://news.bbc.co.uk/go/pr/fr/-/2/hi/technology/3641895.stm

Beech, A. R., Elliott, I. A., Birgden, A., & Findlater, D. (2008). The Internet and child sexual offending: A criminological review. Aggression and Violent Behavior, 13, 216–228.

Bennett, J. (2008, December 29). Why she cuts. Newsweek. Retrieved August 26, 2009 from http://www.newsweek.com/id/177135

Bennett, D. (2012). The Challenges Facing Computer Forensics Investigators in Obtaining Information from Mobile Devices for Use in Criminal Investigations. Information Security Journal: A Global Perspective, 21(3), 159-168. Berger v New York, 388 US 41 (1967).

Bermay, F. P., & Godlove, N. (2012). Understanding 21st century cybercrime from the 'common' victim. Criminal Justice Matters, 89(1), 4-5.

Bhattacharjee, Y. (2011, January 31). How a remote town in Romania has become cybercrime central. Wired.

Bizah, S. & Munongo, S. (2017) Mobile Money Users' Challenges. Evidence From Developing Countries. International Journal of Education and Research, Vol. 5 No. 11 November 2017

Blakey, D. (2000). Under the Microscope: Thematic Inspection Report on Scientific and Technical Support. Her Majesty's Inspectorate of Constabulary, United Kingdom.

Blazak, R. (2001). White boys to terrorist men: Target recruitment of Nazi skinheads. American Behavioral Scientist, 44(6), 982–1000.

Blomquist and Brian (1999) FBI's Web Site Socked as Hackers Target Feds. New York Post 2012

Boateng R, Longe O, Mbarika V (2010). Cybercrime and Criminality in Ghana: Its Forms and Implications. Proceedings of the sixteenth Americas Conference on Information Technology, August 12-15, Lima, Peru

Bocij, P., & McFarlane, L. (2003). Cyberstalking: The technology of hate. The Police Journal, 76, 204-221.

Bologna, G. J., & Lindquist, R. J. (1987). Fraud Accounting and Forensic Accounting – New Tools and Techniques. Brisbane: John Wiley & Sons.

Boston College, Chestnut Hills, MA, pp. 107–116. Retrieved August 25, 2009 from http://artsandscience1.concordia.ca/comm/shade/word/Weborexics.pdf

Bowling, B., & Foster, J. (2002). Policing and the Police. In M. Maguire, R. Morgan & R. Reiner (Eds.), The Oxford Handbook of Criminology, 3rd edition. Oxford: Oxford University Press.

Boyle. J. (2007). Foucault in cyberspace: Surveillance, sovereignty, and hardwired censors. University of Cincinnati Law Review, 66(1), 178-183.

Brenner, S. Carrier, B., & Henninger, J. (2004). The Trojan Horse Defense in Cybercrime Cases. Santa Clara Computer and High Technology Law Journal, 21, 1-53.

Brenner, S. W. (2004). Toward a Criminal Law for Cyberspace: A New Model of Law Enforcement? Rutgers Computer and Technology Law Journal, 30, 1-104.

Brenner, S. W. (2008). Cyber threats: The Emerging Fault Lines of the Nation State. New York: Oxford University Press.

Brenner, S. W., & Koops, B.-J. (2004). Approaches to cybercrime jurisdiction. Journal of High Technology Crime, 15(1), 1-46.

Brian Krebs, "Three Worked the Web to Help Terrorists," The Washington Post, July 6, 2007, p. D01.

Broadhurst and Chang (2012) Cybercrime in Asia: Trends and Challenges, Article in SSRN Electronic Journal. February 2012.DOI:10.2139/ssrn.2118322

Broadhurst, R. G. (2006). Developments in the global law enforcement of cyber-crime. Policing: an International Journal of Police Strategies and Management, 29(3), 408-433.

Broadhurst, R. Grabosky, P., Alazab, M., & Chon, S. (2014). Organizations and Cyber Crime: An Analysis of the Nature of Croups engaged in Cyber Crime. International Journal of Cyber Criminology, 8(1), 1-20.

Broadhurst, R., & Davies, S. E. (Eds.) (2009). Policing in Context: An introduction to Police Work in Australia, South Melbourne, Victoria: Oxford University Press.

Bromby, M. (2006). Security against Crime: Technologies for Detecting and Preventing Crime. International Review of Law Computers & Technology, 20, 1-5.

Brooke, J. (2001, December 23). Sex web spun worldwide traps children. The New York Times. Retrieved August 26, 2009 from http://www.nytimes.com/2001/12/23/world/sex-webspun-worldwide-traps-children.html

Brotsky, S. R., & Giles, D. (2007). Inside the "pro-ana" community: A covert online participant observation. Eating Disorders, 15, 93–107.

Brown, C. S. D. (2015). Cyber-Attacks, Retaliation and Risk: Legal and Technical Implications for Nation-States and Private Entities. In J. L. Richet (Ed.), Cybersecurity Policies and Strategies for Cyber warfare Prevention.

Brunst, P., "Terrorism and the Internet: New Threats Posed by Cyberterrorism and Terrorist Use of the Internet," in A War on Terror? : The European Stance on a New Threat, Changing Laws and Human Rights Implications," 2009.

Butler, K. (2017) Security and Privacy Challenges for Mobile Money Applications. Florida Institute for Cybersecurity Research.

Burke, M. & Ijeoma, A. (2013) Influence of social media on social behaviour of post graduate students. A case study of Salford University, United Kingdom. IOSR Journal of Research & Method in Education (IOSR-JRME) Volume 3, Issue 6 (Nov.–Dec. 2013), PP 39-43 www.iosrjournals.org.

Caldwell and Tracey (2011) Ethical hackers: Putting on the white hat. Network Security 2011

Caltagirone, S. (2015, May 22). The Cost of Bad Threat Intelligence. ActiveResponse.org.

Cameron, S. (2015): Investigating and Prosecuting Cyber Crime: Forensic Dependencies and Barriers to Justice, Australian National University, Australia, International Journal of Cyber Criminology Vol 9 Issue 1 January – June 2015

Camilla A. Tabe and Njofie I. Fieze (2018) A CRITICAL DISCOURSE ANALYSIS OF NEWSPAPER HEADLINES

ON THE ANGLOPHONE CRISIS IN CAMEROON. British Journal of English Linguistics, Vol.6, No.3, pp.64-83, May 2018.

Caproni, V. (2011, February 11). Going Dark: Lawful Electronic Surveillance in the Face of New Technologies. Statement by Valerie Caproni, General Counsel Federal Bureau of Investigation, before the House Judiciary Committee, Subcommittee on Crime, Terrorism, and Homeland Security, Washington, D.C. Retrieved on 14th June 2015 from

Carrier, B. D. (2006). Risks of Live Digital Forensic Analysis. Communications of the ACM, 49(2), 56-61.

Casey, E. (2002). Error Uncertainty and Loss in Digital Evidence. International Journal of Digital Evidence, 1(2).

Casey E (2004). Digital Evidence and Computer Crime: St. Louis, MO: Elsevier Press.

Chau, M., & Xu, J. (2007). Mining communities and their relationships in blogs: A study of online hate groups. International Journal of Human-Computer Studies, 65, 57–70.

Christopher, M. (2013). Violence and Popular Music in Nigeria. NCUE Journal of Humanities Vol. 8, pp. 135-148, September 2013.

CIFAS and CIPD (2012): Staff fraud and dishonesty Managing and Mitigating the risk, Guide June 2012.

Collins, A. and Halverson, R. (2010). The second educational revolution: rethinking education in the age of technology: Journal of Computer Assisted Learning, Blackwell Publishing Ltd

Columbus Dispatch. (2006, May 13). Two-edged sword: Web sites of hate groups, terrorists can give authorities the knowledge to stop them. The Columbus Dispatch (Columbus, OH), editorial.

Commonwealth Foundation (2005). Breaking with Business as Usual: Perspectives from civil society in the Commonwealth on the Millennium Development Goals. London: Commonwealth Foundation, 2: 45.

Cordingley and Julian (2004) Code Hacking: A Developer's Guide to Network Security.

Craig Forcese, "Hacked" US Election: Is International Law Silent, Faced with the Clatter of Cyrillic Keyboards? JUST SECURITY (Dec. 16, 2016), https://www.justsecurity.org/35652/hacked-election-international-law-silentfaced-clatter-cyrillic-keyboards/.

David Sanger, U.S. Officials Defend Integrity of Vote, Despite Hacking Fears, N.Y. TIMES (Nov. 25, 2016),http://www.nytimes.com/2016/11/25/us/politics/hacking-russia-election-fears-barack-obama-donaldtrump.html.

Demetriou, C., & Silke, A. (2003). A criminological internet "sting." Experimental evidence of illegal and deviant visits to a website trap. British Journal of Criminology, 43, 213–222.

Depowski, K., & Hart, K. (2006). "Pro-ana" web sites glorify eating disorders. ABC News.

Retrieved August 26, 2009 from http://abcnews.go.com/Health/story?id=2068728&page=1

Deshotels, T. H., & Forsyth, C. J. (2007). Postmodern masculinities and the eunuch. Deviant Behavior, 28, 201–218.

DiGregory K (2000). Fighting Cybercrime-What are the Challenges Facing Europe? Meeting before the European Parliament; United States Department of Justice.

Dohring, N. M. (2009). The Internet's impact on sexuality: A critical review of 15 years of research. Computers in Human Behavior, 25, 1089–1101.

Dooley, J., Pyżalski, J., and Cross, D. (2009). "Cyberbullying versus face-to-face bullying: A theoretical and conceptual review."

Zeitschrift für Psychologie/Journal of Psychology, Vol. 217, No. 4: pp. 182-188.

Donner, J. and Tellez, C. (2008). "Mobile banking and economic development: Linking adoption, impact, and use", Asian Journal of Communication, 18(4), 318-322.

Douglas, K. M., McGarty, C., Bliuc, A.-M., & Lala, G. (2005). Understanding cyberhate: Social competition and social creativity in online white supremacist groups. Social Science Computer Review, 23, 68–76.

Durkin, K. F. (1997). Misuse of the internet by pedophiles: Implications for law enforcement and probation practice. Federal Probation, 61(3), 14-19.

Durkin, K. F., & Bryant, C. D. (1999). Propagandizing pederasty: A thematic analysis of on-line exculpatory accounts of unrepentant pedophiles. Deviant Behavior, 20, 103–127.

Durkin, K., Forsyth, C. J., & Quinn, J. F. (2006). Pathological Internet communities: A new direction for sexual deviance research in a postmodern era. Sociological Spectrum, 26(6), 595–606.

Ehimen O, Bola A (2010). Cybercrime in Nigeria; Bus Intelligence J,3:93-98

Eichenwald, K. (2006, August 21). From their own online world, pedophiles extend their reach. The New York Times. Retrieved August 26, 2009 from http://query.nytimes.com/gst/fullpage.html?res=9C02E3DF123EF932A1575BC0A960 9C8B63

Elliott, I. A., & Beech, A. R. (2009). Understanding online child pornography use: Applying sexual offense theory to internet offenders. Aggression and Violent Behavior, 14, 180–193.

Eric Lipton, David E. Sanger and Scott Shane, The Perfect Weapon: How Russian Cyberpower Invaded the U.S., N.Y. TIMES (Dec. 13, 2016), http://www.nytimes.com/2016/12/13/us/politics/russia-hack-election-dnc.html;

Farhood N. Dezfoli et al (2013) Digital Forensic Trends and Future. International Journal of Cyber-Security and Digital Forensics (IJCSDF) 2(2): 48-76

Freeman et al (1997). At Large: The Strange Case of the World's Biggest Internet Invasion. New York: Simon & Schuster.

Fick, J. (2009). Cybercrime in South Africa: Investigating and prosecuting cybercrime and the benefits of public-private partnerships, Council of Europe octopus interface conference cooperation against cybercrime 10-11 March 2009, Strasbourg, France.

Foderaro, L. (2010). Private Moment Made Public, Then a Fatal Jump. The New York Times (NYT), 09/29/2010.

Funk, A. (2016) Drones in Contemporary Warfare: The Implications for Human Rights http://blogs.lse.ac.uk/humanrights/2016/07/07/dronesincontemporarywarfare-theimplicationsforhumanrights/

Gerstenfeld, P. B., Grant, D. R., & Chiang, C.-P. (2003). Hate online: A content analysis of extremist websites. Analyses of Social Issues and Public Policy, 3(1), 29–44.

Giles, D. C. (2006). Constructing identities in cyberspace: The case of eating disorders. British Journal of Social Psychology, 45, 463–477.

Glaser, J., Dixit, J., & Green, D. P. (2002). Studying hate crime with the Internet: What makes racists advocate racial violence? Journal of Social Issues, 58(1), 177–193.

Goffman, E. (1963). Stigma: Notes on the management of spoiled identity. Englewood Cliffs, NJ: Prentice Hall.

Granville and Johanna (2003). Dot.Con: The Dangers of Cyber Crime and a Call for Proactive Solutions. Australian Journal of Politics and History.

Greene, D. 2015. Drone Vision. Surveillance & Society 13(2): 233 249.http://www.surveillance-and-society.org.

Grov, C. (2004). "Make me your death slave": Men who have sex with men and use the internet to intentionally spread HIV. Deviant Behavior, 25(4), 329.

Heatherly, Michael C. "Drones: The American Controversy." Journal of Strategic Security7, no. 4 (2014) : 25-37.

Herhat, J. (2011). Cyber Crime a Growing Challenge for Government.

Hirschi, T., & Gottfredson, M. (1990). A general theory of crime. In F. Cullen & R. Agnew (Eds.), Criminological Theory: Past to Present Essential Readings. New York, NY: Oxford University Press

Horn P (2006). It's Time to Arrest Cybercrime; Business Week Online http://www.businessweek.com/technology/content/feb2006/tc20060 202_832554.htm

Human Rights Watch (2013) "Between a Drone and Al-Qaeda" The Civilian Cost of US Targeted Killings in Yemen.

Jack McDonald (2018) Drones and the European Union: Prospects for a Common Future. Chatham House

Jenkins, P. (2001). Beyond tolerance: Child pornography on the Internet. New York: New York University Press.

Jialun Qin et al., "Analyzing Terror Campaigns on the Internet: Technical Sophistication, Content Richness and Web Interactivity," International Journal of Human-Computer Studies, November 1, 2006, vol. 65, p.71–84.

Joinson, A. N. (2005). Deviance and the internet: New challenges for social science. Social Science Computer Review, 23(1), 5–7.

Katherine M. G. (2012) An Examination of Cybercrime and Cybercrime Research: Self-control and Routine Activity Theory, Arizona State University, 1 March 2012

King, J., & Stones, W. (2013). Rise in negative behavior among middle school and college students in Sydney. Australian Journal of Sociological Studies, 13-19.

Kiragu, J. (2015). The negative influence of social media on our communities. Journal of Family Studies.

Krone, T. (2004). A typology of online child pornography offending. Trends and Issues in Crime and Criminal Justice, 279, 1–6.

Lanning, K. V. (2001). Child molesters: A behavioral analysis, fourth edition. Arlington, VA: National Center for Missing and Exploited Children. Retrieved August 27, 2009 from http://www.missingkids.com/en_US/publications/NC70.pdf

Langman, L. (2003). Culture, identity and hegemony: The body in a global age. Current Sociology, 51, 223–247.

Laws, R. D., & O'Donohue, W. (1997). Fundamental issues in sexual deviance. In D. R. Laws, & W. O'Donohue (Eds.), Sexual deviance. Theory, assessment and treatment. (pp. 1-21). New York: The Guilford Press.

Lee, E., & Leets, L. (2002). Persuasive storytelling by hate groups online: Examining its effects on adolescents. American Behavioral Scientist, 45(6), 927–957.

Lillian Ablon et al (2014) Markets for Cybercrime Tools and Stolen Data Hackers' Bazaar, national security research division, 2014.

Longe O, Chiemeke S (2008). Cybercrime and Criminality in Nigeria- What Roles are Internet Access Points in Playing? European J. Soc. Sci. 6 (4): 132-139.

Matt Flegenheimer and Michael Barbaro, Donald Trump is Elected President in Stunning Repudiation of the Establishment, N.Y. TIMES (Nov. 9, 2016), http://www.nytimes.com/2016/11/09/us/politics/hillary-clintondonald-trump-president.html

McAfee Inc (2009). McAfee Reveals the Riskiest Web Domains to Surf and Search, McAfee's Third Annual Report.

McCullagh, Declan, 'Military Worried About Web Leaks.' CNET News 16 January 2003, available at: http://news.com. com/2100-1023-981057.html.

McDonald, S., Horstmann, N., Strom, J., & Pope, W. (2009). The Impact of the Internet on Deviant Behavior and Deviant Communities. Institute for Homeland Security Solution. Applied Research. Focused Result

Mehlum, L. (2000). The internet, suicide, and suicide prevention. Crisis, 21(4), 186–188.

Mesch, G. S. (2009). Social bonds and Internet pornographic exposure among adolescents. Journal of Adolescence, 32, 601–618.

Mforgham S (2010). Cameroon to set Up Cyber Police Force; Africa News.com. http://www.africanews.com/site/Cameroon_to_ set_up_cyber_police _force/list_messages

Mforgham S (2010). Cameroon:22 Internet Fraudsters Arrested, Africa News,

http://www.africanews.com/site/Cameroon_22_Internet_ fraudsters_ arrested/list_messages

Mitchell, K. J., & Ybarra, M. L. (2007). Online behavior of youth who engage in self-harm provides clues for preventive intervention. Preventive Medicine, 45, 392–396.

Mosima E (2009). Fighting Trans-National Crime Police Officers Mobilized, Cameroon Tribune, http://allafrica.com/ stories/200909090372.html

MUIA, W. (2016) Influence Of Social Media On Deviant Behaviour Among Secondary School Students In Langata Sub-County, Nairobi County, Kenya. University of Nairobi.

Munongo, S. & Bizah, D. (2017). Mobile Money Users' Challenges. Evidence From Developing Countries. International Journal of Education and Research, Vol. 5 No. 11 November 2017.

Mutume G (2007). Organised Crime Targets Weak African States, 21(2) African Renewal, 3.

NordiskaAfrkainstitutet (2001). ASSOCIATIONAL LIFE IN AFRICAN CITIES: Popular Responses to the Urban Crisis

Odumesi (2014) A Socio-technological analysis of cybercrime and cyber security in Nigeria. International Journal of Sociology and Anthropology vol.6 (3), pp.116-125, March, 2014

Ojedokun, A. (2005). The Evolving Sophistication of Internet Abuses in Africa: the International Information and Library Review

Oji, O. and Chukwuemeka, E (1999). Applied Social and Behavioural Research: Guidlines for Thesis writing. Enugu: John Jacob's Classic Publisher

Okeshola, B. & Adeta, K. (2013). The Nature, Causes and Consequences of Cyber Crime in Tertiary Institutions in Zaria-Kaduna State, Nigeria. American International Journal of Contemporary Research, Vol. 3 No. 9; September 2013.

Olowu D (2009). Cyber-Crimes and the Boundaries of Domestic Legal Responses: Case for an Inclusionary Framework for Africa, 2009(1) J. Inform. Law Technol. (JILT), http://go.warwick.ac.uk/jilt/2009_1/olowu.

Omolo, J. (2014). Trends of antisocial behavior among minors in Nairobi populous estates: A study of Karen and Runda estates. Journal of Family Studies, 13(4) 165-176.

Oriola TA (2005). Advance Fee Fraud on the Internet: Nigeria's Regulatory Response, 21 Computer Law and Security Report.

Particia, M., & Ndung'u, J. (2014). The erosion of our social morality among high-end family settings. Journal of Family Management.

Paulauskas, R. (2013) Is Causal Attribution of Sexual Deviance the Source of Thinking Errors? International Education Studies; Vol. 6, No. 4; 2013.

Peterkins Manyong (2009) Analysis: Of Scammers and other Website Predators, December 18, 2009.

Pondi, E. (2011) Sexual Harassment and Deontology in the University Milieu. Edition CLE 2011 Prostitution taking over Yaoundé. Cameroonweb, General News of Mon, 13 July 2015.

Postal and Telecommunications Regulatory Authority of Zimbabwe (Potraz). (2014). Postal And Telecommunications Sector Performance Report Third Quarter 2014.

Quinn, J. F. & Forsyth, C. J. (2005). Describing sexual behavior in the era of the internet: A typology for empirical research. Deviant Behavior, 26, 191–207.

Reed, B. (2007, January 15). Cutting on increase in teens, say experts. The MetroWest Daily News, Framingham, MA. Retrieved August 26, 2009 from http://www.metrowestdailynews.com/homepage/8999002596093984767

Rege, A. (2009) what's Love Got to Do with It? Exploring Online Dating Scams and Identity Fraud. International Journal of Cyber Criminology Vol 3 Issue 2 July – December 2009

Reyes, N. (2016) Women and Terrorism: Challenging Traditional Gender Roles. Undergraduate Journal of Political Science, Vol. 1, No. 1, Spring 2016, Pp. 119–124

Ribadu, E. (2007), Cyber Crime and Commercial Fraud; A Nigerian Perspective. A paper presented at the Modern Law for Global Commerce, Vienna 9th – 12th July.

Rivituso, G. (2012). "Cyberbullying: an exploration of the lived experiences and the psychological impact of victimization among college students an interpretive phenomenological analysis" Education Doctoral Theses, Paper 21.

Rogers, M., Smoak, N., & Liu, J. (2006). Self-reported deviant computer behavior. Deviant Behavior, 27(3), 245–268.

Roland Paulauskas (2013) Is Causal Attribution of Sexual Deviance the Source of Thinking Errors? International Education Studies; Vol. 6, No. 4; 2013

SCHROEDER, R. (2016). The Globalization of On-Screen Sociability: Social Media and Tethered Togetherness. International Journal of Communication 10(2016), 5626–5643

Scott, K. (2000, February 7). Voluntary amputee ran disability site. The Guardian, UKNews. Retrieved August 26, 2009 from http://www.guardian.co.uk/uk/2000/feb/07/kirstyscott2

Sesan, G. (2010), The New Security War.http://www.pcworld.com/article/122492/the_new_security_war.htm#tk.mod-rel

Setiadi F. et al (2012) An Overview of the Development Indonesia National Cyber Security

Shade, L. R. (2003, June). Weborexics: The ethical issues surrounding pro-ana websites. Proceedings of the Fifth International Conference on Computer Ethics–Philosophical Enquiry.

Sher, L. (2000). The internet, suicide, and human mental functions. Canadian Journal of Psychiatry, 45, 297. 11

Skye, J. (2012). Cyber Bullying Statistics. Love to Know Safety

Social Bakers. (2013). Social Bakers 2013: a year in review. Retrieved 07 19, 2015, from Social Bakers: http://www.socialbakers.com/blog/2068-socialbakers-2013-a-year-in-review

Stack, S., Wasserman, I., & Kern, R. (2004). Adult social bonds and use of internet

Spyridon Samonas (2013) Insider fraud and routine activity theory, originally Presented at 12th Annual Security Conference, 11 April 2013 Las Vegas, Nevada, Available in LSE Research Online May 2013.

Sukumar A. and Col. Sharma R. (2016) The Cyber Command: Upgrading India's National Security Architecture.

Tabe, A. & Fieze, I. (2018). A Critical Discourse Analysis of Newspaper Headlines on the Anglophone Crisis in Cameroon. British Journal of English Linguistics, Vol.6, No.3, pp.64-83, May 2018.

The Bureau of Investigative Journalism. 2011. "The Bush Years: Pakistan Strikes 2004-2009", Get the Data: Drone Wars, August 10. Accessed March 14, 2014: http://www.thebureauinvestigates.com/2011/08/10/the-bush-years-2004-2009/.

The Bureau of Investigative Journalism. 2014. "Casualty Estimates," Get the Data: Drone Wars, http://www.thebureauinvestigates.com/category/projects/drones/drones-graphs/ Accessed August 6, 2014:http://www.thebureauinvestigates.com/2011/08/10/the-bush-years-2004-2009/.

Todd, A. B. (2009). Children, adolescents, and the media. Sage.

Van Der Leun, G. (2001, June 24). Twilight zone of the id. Time Magazine. Retrieved August 26, 2009 from http://www.time.com/time/magazine/article/0,9171,133825,00.html?iid=digg_share

Virkus, S. (2008). Use of Web 2.0 technologies in LIS education: experiences at Tallinn University, Estonia. Program: Electronic Library and Information Systems, 42(3), 262-274.

Wacka, J. (2014) Understanding and Investigating Cyber Criminality and Terrorist Acts. A Practical Approach for Law Enforcement Agents and the Judiciary, University of Buea, 13 November 2014

Wall, T. and Monahan, T.: Surveillance and violence from afar: The politics of drones and liminal security-scapes, Theor. Criminol., 15, 239–254, 2011.

Weimann, G. (2006). Virtual disputes: The use of the internet for terrorist debates. Studies in Conflict & Terrorism, 29(7), 623–639.

Weimann, G. (2004b). How Modern Terrorism Uses the Internet, Special Report (United

States Institute of Peace), 116.

Weitzer, R. (2011) Legalizing Prostitution. From Illicit Vice to Lawful Business.

Whitlock, J. L., Powers, J. L., & Eckenrode, J. (2006). The virtual cutting edge: The internet and adolescent self-injury. Development Psychology, 42(3), 407–417.

Wilhelm and Douglas (2010) Professional Penetration Testing. Syngress Press. EC-Council. eccouncil.org

Wolf, C. (2009, June 17). The hatemongers' new tool: The Internet. Retrieved August 25, 2009 from http://www.cbsnews.com/stories/2009/06/16/opinion/main5092743.shtml

Conferences, Thesis and News

Agbor Laura Cyber Criminality as a Crime in Cameroon (2016). Thesis University of Buea, Cameroon.

Anthony Mormino (2017) Insurance and the Rise of the Drones. Casualty Actuarial Society, Spring Meeting, Toronto.

Bekali Eposi, "Women's Involvement in Cyber Crime and its Effects on their status: The Case Study of Buea Municipality",(2017). Thesis University of Buea, Cameroon.

Biggs, S., & Vidalis, S. (2009,). Cloud computing: the impact on digital forensic investigations. Paper presented at the International Conference for Internet Technology and Secured Transactions (ICITST). IEEE (pp. 1-6).

Biko, G. (2016). Understanding Cyber terrorism and mobile intrusion. Conference at Mansel Hotel, Yaounde by Smart Hacking School.

Business in Cameroon (2016). Cyber-criminality wreaking havoc in Cameroon, according to Antic.

CAJ News Africa (2016). Cameroon in Catch 22 capture cybercriminals.

Institute for Homeland Security Solutions (2009) The Impact of the Internet on Deviant Behavior and Deviant Communities.

Juliet K. TUMUZOIRE (2016) Challenges and Opportunities for Mobile Money. MTN UGANDA Region - East Africa

Peter Steiner, page 61 of July 5, 1993 issue of The New Yorker, (Vol.69 (LXIX) no. 20).

Pew Research Center, "Global Opposition to U.S. Surveillance and Drones, but Limited Harm to America's Image," Pew Research Center Global Attitudes & Trends website, 14 July 2014, accessed 1 September 2015, http://www.pewglobal.org/2014/07/14/global-opposition-to-u-ssurveillance-and-drones-but-limited-harm-to-americas-image/

Putin's Revenge, POLITICO MAGAZINE (Dec. 2016), http://www.politico.com/magazine/story/2016/12/russia-putin-hack-dnc-clinton-election-2016-cold-war.

Quirk Cort, Mary Elizabeth, "The Power of Lyrical Protest: Examining the Rhetorical Function of Protest Songs in the 2000s" (2013). Thesis. Rochester Institute of Technology.

Saron, M. Obia "Cyber Criminality As An Emergent Security Challenge in Cameroon", (2016). Thesis Pan African Institute for Development-West Africa (PAID-WA)

Index

A

Al-Qaida 97

Anwar al-Awlaki 103

B

Biometric Classification 59

Biometric Patterns viii, 60

Biometric Strategy viii, 61

Boko-Haram cyber-attack 25

C

Challenges of Criminal Investigations 23

Character of Crime in Africa 9

Child sexual exploitation 27

Civil Aviation Organisation (ICAO) 62

Computer Incident Response Team (CIRT) 28, 31

Cyberbullying viii, 49, 114, 121

Cybercriminals 12

Modus Operandi 12

Profiling 15

Cyber deviance in the music industry 44

Cyberespionage 38

Cyber-risk Management Programs 27

Cyberstalking 8, 9, 110

D

Department for Children, Schools and Families 30

Department of Homeland Security (DHS) 26

Deviant behaviour 10

DHS Cyber Security Division 26

Domain Name System 65

E

Economic and Financial Crime Commission 31, 33

Electronic funds transfer (EFT) 18

F

Federal Bureau of Investigation 79

Federal Network Security 26

Financial crime viii, 77

Forensic investigation viii, 67

Fraud Reporting Centre 30

H

Hacking of accounts and skimming 81

Hate ideologies 10

I

Identity theft on mobile money 81

India iii, iv

Information Technology (IT) 17

Internet Protocol (IP) 7

Internet Service Providers (ISP) 63

Internet Watch Foundation 30

M

Misha Glenny 6

Mobile Money Accounts 83

N

National Agency for Financial Investigations 31

National Cyber Security Division 26

National Cyberspace Response

System 26

National Fraud Authority 30

National Fraud Intelligence Bureau 31

Nigerian Police Force 33

O

Offensive content 81

Online Protection Centre 30

Organization of the Islamic Conference 29

R

Robert K. Merton 11

Rutgers University 50

S

Sakawa 32, 68

Salafi group in FATA. *See* Amr bil ma'ruf Wa Nahi An Al-Munkar

Scammer 13, 14, 19

Serious Organized Crime Agency 31

Sexual Deviance 47, 121, 122

Simbox 12

Stanley Mark Rifkin Case 82

T

The constructive theory 21, 22

The Triangular Theory of Crimes
19

Three Stage Model of Cybercrimi-
nality 71

Thugry 12

Transmission Control Protocol
(TCP) 7

Typology of Crimes 7

  Carders or card cloned 7

  Cyberstalking 8

  Internet dating and romance
    scam 8

  Malware 7

  Phishing 8

U

UK Council for Child Internet
Safety 30

CPSIA information can be obtained
at www.ICGtesting.com
Printed in the USA
LVHW091756180121
676805LV00004B/197